DECODING GEN Z

101 LESSONS GENERATION Z WILL TEACH CORPORATE AMERICA, MARKETERS & MEDIA

INSIGHTS DIRECTLY FROM THE
MINDS AND MOUTHS OF GEN ZERS

MARK BEAL

D1247238

Published by Mark Beal Media, LLC
Toms River, New Jersey

Editing: Antonia Attardo
Cover Design: Evan Carroll

ISBN: 9781724080882
First Printing: 2018 Printed in the United States of America

Decoding Gen Z: 101 Lessons Generation Z Will Teach Corporate America, Marketers & Media is available for bulk orders, special promotions and premiums.

Z Talks for Your Company or Organization:
Mark Beal has a proprietary panel of Gen Zers across the nation who are available to bring this book to life via a series of "Z Talks" to companies, organizations and associations in which they will deliver real-time information and insights that can inform your next campaign, content marketing production or workplace culture initiative.

For details, call +1.848.992.0391 or email markbeal@markbealmedia.com

This book is dedicated to Generation Z, a generation that will change the world; challenge the status quo; transform the way we work and socialize; revolutionize industries, corporations, brands and organizations; and inspire other generations for many years to come. I am privileged and honored to be able to collaborate with members of Gen Z as a university professor and learn as much from them as I teach.

ACKNOWLEDGEMENTS

In 2013, I started teaching in the School of Communication at Rutgers University. Since that time, I have taught and mentored more than 1,000 college students in courses with a focus on public relations and marketing. The students at Rutgers University and across the nation inspired me to author my first book in 2017 titled, *101 Lessons They Never Taught You In College*. The book featured 101 answers to the many questions students asked me regarding how to transition from college to a career. The book was so well received by media nationwide that I decided to write a second book crowdsourcing current college students and recent graduates on the advice they would give to incoming college freshman. *101 Lessons They Never Taught You In High School About Going To College* was published in early 2018 and received even more attention from media and consumers than my first book. With that, I was asked repeatedly during media interviews what the topic of my next "101 Lessons" book would be. It was at this same time that I was starting to collaborate with the student-run public relations agency at Montclair State University, Hawk Communications, and I was inspired once again.

As I collaborated with the Montclair State University students and continued to teach the Rutgers University students, I immersed myself in Generation Z. Each morning, the first thing I would do is conduct an online search for any new Gen Z insights or data. I soon learned that nearly every day a new Gen Z study or survey was released somewhere around the world. Every new piece of research was intended to advise older generations that Gen Z was coming soon, and they need to prepare. The fact is, Gen Z is already here, and most companies and brand marketers are just starting to shift their primary focus from millennials to Gen Z. With that, Decoding *Gen Z: 101 Lessons Generation Z Will Teach Corporate America, Marketers & Media*, was born.

I first want to thank all the Gen Zers, recent college graduates, current college students and current high school students, who took time by phone, text and email to provide me endless insights about Gen Z, their social media routines, media consumption preferences, technology trends and wishes for the workplace. They include Sabrina Araullo, Montclair State University; Antonia Attardo, Rutgers University; Summer Beal, East Stroudsburg University; Matt Boyce, Toms River North High School; Rachel Boyce, Stockton University; Cole Butchen, Cornell University; Zoe Butchen, University of Connecticut; David Casadonte, Fordham University; Courtney Copeland, Rutgers University; Paige Daly, University of New Haven; Brendan Deal, Monroe Township High School; Jenna DeMato, Rutgers University; Derek Drotman, Penn State University; Elissa Edwards, SUNY Old Westbury; Shelby Fong, Rutgers University; Carly Galasso, Rutgers University; Kelsey Geisenheimer, Syracuse University; Christian Glew, University of Alabama; Christina Hamdan, University of Delaware; Sierra Haney, The College of New Jersey; Quinn Heinrich, Loyola Marymount University; Melissa Jannuzzi, Rutgers University; Ryan Jannuzzi, Rutgers University; Sophia Kazee, University of Pittsburgh; Sophie Kleinberg, The Beacon School; Micah Lebowitz, Rutgers University; Gabrielle Liguori, Rutgers University; Kaitlyn Matthews, Rutgers University; Sally Meli, Wagner College; Stephanie Michael, Montclair State University; Mike Morra, Manhattan College; Jessica Ortega, Montclair State University; Jake Panus, Fairfield Ludlowe High School; Amanda Peacock, Montclair State University; Alexa Restaino, Rutgers University; Kylie Rissmiller, East Stroudsburg University; Alyssa Rivers, Rutgers University; Amanda Romano, Rutgers University; Ashley Rose, University of Mississippi; Ryan Rose, Rutgers University; Thomas Saacks, Calvert Hall College

High School; Carmen Sclafani, Rutgers University; Brooke Stern, Cornell University; Austin Sommerer, Penn State University; Ryan Stiesi, Rutgers University; Rahima Tokhi, Rutgers University; Hailey Winnicky, East Stroudsburg University; and Katelyn Woebse, Montclair State University.

I would like to thank my wife, Michele, for 30-years of love-filled collaboration. If it was not for your selflessness, I would never be able to pursue my passion projects including authoring this book and the time that is required late at night and on weekends to conduct extensive research and write. It's all the sacrifices that you have made over the past three decades that have allowed me to thoroughly enjoy careers as a marketer, professor and author.

Michele and I are Gen Xers, and we are very proud of our family: our son, Drew, and his wife, Huda, both millennials, who always lend their support to me behind-the scenes for my passion projects including this book and my 101 Lessons podcast series, and the proud parents of our grandson, Marc, one of the youngest members of Gen Alpha; our daughter, Meghan, a millennial, who teaches the youngest Gen Zers each and every day and who inspires me with not only her approach to living life to the fullest and making this world a better place, but for her parenting of her son and our oldest grandson, Luke, another member of Gen Alpha, who will influence me one day to write a book about his and Marc's generation; and our daughter, Summer, among the oldest members of Gen Z, who not only inspired me to write this book but also contributed to it on a daily basis for many months with her endless amount of Gen Z insights, information and terminology as she was making her own transition from college to a career like so many other Gen Zers who graduated college in 2018.

My teaching and writing is built on a foundation of nearly 30 years of marketing in collaboration with Tony Signore, Bryan Harris and John Liporace. Since 1988, when I first interned for Tony and Bryan, I have had the honor of collaborating with them in developing and executing marketing campaigns for some of the world's leading consumer brands and for that, I am extremely thankful to each of them for their inspiration, motivation and partnership.

I would like to thank Stan Phelps, author of the Goldfish series of books and keynote speaker. In addition to Stan inspiring me and mentoring me as I authored my first two books, it was Stan who came up with the Decoding Gen Z title for this book over a great Italian dinner in Brick, NJ at one of my favorite restaurants at the Jersey Shore, Via Veneto, while Stan was making his way from speaking opportunities in Europe to a keynote speech in Atlantic City, NJ to catch a flight in New York.

I would like to thank Evan Carroll for translating all my Gen Z content into a book that will provide valuable insights for corporate America, marketers, media and so many others for many years to come. Thank you for the time and expertise you dedicated to the layout and design of this book and my two previous books.

I would like to thank one of my Rutgers University students, Antonia Attardo, for dedicating a significant portion of her summer of 2018 to this book including lending her insights, recruiting fellow Gen Zers to participate, reviewing and sourcing all references, editing and writing the foreword. I believed from the moment that I started writing this book that it was mandatory for me to collaborate with a Gen Zer and Antonia did exceptional work.

I would like to thank all the Gen Zers at Montclair State University's student-run public relations, Hawk Communications, who I have the privilege of collaborating with as they evolve their agency to be among the best in the nation at the university level.

I would like to thank Keith Strudler, the director of the School of Communication and Media at Montclair State University and Kelly Whiteside, an assistant professor, sports media and journalism, also at Montclair State University, who invited me to collaborate with their student-run public relations agency, Hawk Communications.

I would like to thank my colleagues at Rutgers University. If it wasn't for the phone call they made to me in 2013, I never would have had the opportunity to teach courses at the same university I graduated from in 1989 and more importantly, be inspired by the incredible Gen Z students at Rutgers who teach me more about their generation than I could ever learn elsewhere. Special thanks to all the faculty at Rutgers who I have the privilege of calling colleagues including, but not limited to, Brian Householder, Steve Miller, Richard Dool, Jack Grasso, Ken Hunter, Mike Finkelstein and Art Berke.

I would like to thank photographer and friend, David Dodds, for taking the time to photograph me for this book and my previous two books.

Finally, I would like to thank all the "givers" in my professional and social networks. Every time I publish a new book or release a new podcast, you are the first to share with the rest of the world via your own channels and advocate on my behalf. There is nothing more powerful than having a network of amazing people who unselfishly take the time to share, promote and amplify my passion projects. I am eternally grateful to each and every one of you. Thank you.

FROM THE MINDS & MOUTHS OF GEN Z

"Our generation is being heard for sure. Gen Z will change the world."

CHRISTINA HAMDAN, UNIVERSITY OF DELAWARE, CLASS OF 2019

"We are openly discussing a variety of issues and creating a Gen Z movement. I participated in my first march this year and it was loud, empowering and full of energy and I can't wait to do it again with other students from my generation."

JAKE PANUS, FAIRFIELD LUDLOWE HIGH SCHOOL, CLASS OF 2022

"If you are a brand marketer, you need to get ahead of Gen Z. In other words, you need to interview us and listen closely and understand what trends we are forecasting six to 12 months into the future. We move faster than any generation before us and if you are planning some sort of marketing campaign today to engage Gen Z, there is a good chance it will be old news by the time you go to market with it unless you get ahead of the Gen Z curve."

DEREK DROTMAN, PENN STATE UNIVERSITY CLASS OF 2020

"Brands need to stand for something that is not only important in today's culture and society if they want to have a long-term relationship with Gen Z, but the brand's purpose must be sharable with our way of living."

STEPHANIE MICHAEL, MONTCLAIR STATE UNIVERSITY, CLASS OF 2019

"My ultimate goal is to be able to work in a field that I'm passionate about, and when people give you the space to be creative and think outside of the box, you're more likely to invest your time and effort into something you truly care about...In the workplace, there needs to be room to foster new ideas, growth, and encouragement for people to pursue their passions, so they can contribute without worry of consequences."

ALYSSA RIVERS, RUTGERS UNIVERSITY, CLASS OF 2020

"Large corporations can benefit from having communities that foster real connections and shared passions. Through smaller interest groups, we gain a greater sense of belonging."

COLE BUTCHEN, CORNELL UNIVERSITY, CLASS OF 2019

"When searching for jobs, we are looking for companies that offer flexibility when it comes to where they allow us to work and at what hours...In our tech-centric way of working and living, we realize that our work will surround us 24/7, so we are seeking employers who have future-forward mindsets and offer the opportunity to work remotely and even non-traditional hours."

AUSTIN SOMMERER, PENN STATE UNIVERSITY, CLASS OF 2017

"Anyone can accept an assignment, but Gen Z wants to go beyond the tactical instructions and understand the ultimate goal in accomplishing the task."

KELSEY GEISENHEIMER, SYRACUSE UNIVERSITY, CLASS OF 2018

"Please don't invite me just to do the grunt work early on in a project or presentation and then ignore me when it comes time for the big reveal... If you believe I can deliver value in the first or second phase of program development than offer me the opportunity to be part of the team that is going to see the project through completion

SIERRA HANEY, THE COLLEGE OF NEW JERSEY, CLASS OF 2018

"As we enter the workforce, we are bringing these tools and technology with us and we won't hesitate to recommend anything that helps get the job completed more efficiently especially if we work with teams that span multiple time zones."

QUINN HEINRICH, LOYOLA MARYMOUNT UNIVERSITY, CLASS OF 2018

"Whether you call it peer-to-peer advising or peer mentorship, we are highly motivated when we are paired with other Gen Zers on projects, programs and assignments because we don't want to let each other down."

CARMEN SCLAFANI, RUTGERS UNIVERSITY, CLASS OF 2019

"Finding someone who I can trust to guide me through that first critical year or two out of college is much more important to my long-term career success than an authoritative manager who is focused solely on the day-to-day tactical execution."

ANTONIA ATTARDO, RUTGERS UNIVERSITY, CLASS OF 2019

"We are a generation that is seeking spontaneous experiences. I never know where the next text message may take me."

HAILEY WINNICKY, EAST STROUDSBURG UNIVERSITY, CLASS OF 2019

"Communities or networks of people who share common interests...is very important to our generation...these communities not only feed our passions, they give us balance in our lives, especially when it comes to work life balance

JESSICA ORTEGA, MONTCLAIR STATE UNIVERSITY, CLASS OF 2019

"From customizing my own music playlist for every mood I am feeling to designing my own sneakers to personalizing my watches, marketers who will successfully engage with Gen Z will offer options for us to customize and personalize their products and services."

ALEXA RESTAINO, RUTGERS UNIVERSITY, CLASS OF 2019

"When Gen Zers consider a brand or making a purchase, we conduct extensive research and our friends and family are by far our greatest influence."

KATELYN WOEBSE, MONTCLAIR STATE UNIVERSITY, CLASS OF 2020

"We turn to apps for everything from entertainment and fun to protecting us and getting us to our destination in the most-timely way."

ELISSA EDWARDS, SUNY OLD WESTBURY CLASS, OF 2020

"Advanced degrees and continuing to educate ourselves will only become increasingly more important for me and my generation as we join the workforce."

CARLY GALASSO, RUTGERS UNIVERSITY CLASS OF 2018

"Twitch, the online live streaming video platform for video gamers, is huge and only getting bigger as eSports evolves and grows...With that, there is a whole new set of influencers, specifically gaming influencers with massive followings."

THOMAS SAACKS, CALVERT HALL COLLEGE HIGH SCHOOL, CLASS OF 2022

"We are not at a tipping point yet, but there is a growing dislike by Gen Zers when it comes to the blatant advertising on our favorite social media channels."

SABRINA ARAULLO, MONTCLAIR STATE UNIVERSITY, CLASS OF 2018

"Brands should seek to develop clever and cool concepts with Gen Z relevance. If executed properly, my generation will not only be engaged in the moment, but we will eagerly share the experiences with our friends and followers... My recommendation to every brand marketer who is looking to engage and win over Gen Zers for the next decade is to recruit their own diverse Gen Z panel. The panel's thoughts and feedback will help ensure organizations' inspired marketing innovations are not only on brand, but in fact, on target."

MICAH LEBOWITZ, RUTGERS UNIVERSITY, CLASS OF 2018

"We are not going to take time out of our day to go to an actual store to shop when we can make the same purchase using our mobile phone while we are commuting to our internship or in between classes...Other generations may consider us lazy, but we value our time tremendously and we look to accomplish all tasks in the most efficient way to get them done without wasting time."

ASHLEY ROSE, UNIVERSITY OF MISSISSIPPI, CLASS OF 2020

"Group chats, especially through applications like GroupMe, have made communication with others so much easier."

JENNA DEMATO, RUTGERS UNIVERSITY, CLASS OF 2019

"We want to collaborate with others face-to-face in a meaningful way to learn, grow and evolve... and in the process, make our communities and world a better place to live."

SUMMER BEAL, EAST STROUDSBURG UNIVERSITY, CLASS OF 2018

Collaboration with a diverse group of people, experiences and mindsets is very important to us."

RYAN STIESI, RUTGERS UNIVERSITY, CLASS OF 2019

"As for watching network television, Gen Zers undoubtedly prefer watching their content on streaming platforms such as Netflix, Hulu and Amazon."

DAVID CASADONTE, FORDHAM UNIVERSITY, CLASS OF 2018

"We expect brands to market to us, but if they truly want to engage us, they need to do it in an authentic Gen Z kind of way and inject their brand into our lives across work, friends, passions, causes and social media."

MELISSA JANNUZZI, RUTGERS UNIVERSITY, CLASS OF 2017

"I have a fascination with this movement away from social media and technology. There is this moving desire for more immersive experiences."

MIKE MORRA, MANHATTAN COLLEGE, CLASS OF 2017

"We are a generation of entrepreneurs."

SOPHIE KLEINBERG, THE BEACON SCHOOL, CLASS OF 2021

TABLE OF CONTENTS

PART I: GEN Z GLOSSARY

PART II: LOWKEY/HIGHKEY MOODS OF GEN Z

PART III: SPILLING THE TEA
ON GEN Z AT THE WORKPLACE

PART IV: SLIDING INTO
GEN Z'S MEDIA PREFERENCES

PART V: THE WAVE FOR BRAND MARKETERS

PART VI: THE DOPE ON
TECH, APPS & SOCIAL MEDIA

PART VII: PEEPING THE
GEN Z TWEET ON TRENDS & TOPICS

FOREWORD

BY ANTONIA ATTARDO

As I approach my final year at Rutgers University, I begin to reflect on all that I have learned, the wonderful people I have met and the professors that have motivated and inspired me along the way. Author Mark Beal has served as a professor, mentor and friend of mine throughout my early career. I was honored when he asked me to write the foreword for his book, *Decoding Gen Z: 101 Lessons Generation Z Will Teach Corporate America, Marketers & Media*.

As a Gen Zer, I am immersed in the culture of my generation. For this book, I was able to analyze and infuse insights regarding the impact Gen Z will have on the workplace, media and marketers.

I hear cynics every day, grumbling about how members of Gen Z always have their heads in their phones, or how Gen Z is lazy and doesn't want to work, or Gen Z speaks how they text. Yet, *Decoding Gen Z: 101 Lessons Generation Z Will Teach Corporate America, Marketers & Media* defies these cavalier comments and taps into the tremendous potential of this generation.

Mark's previous books, *101 They Never Taught You in College* and *101 Lessons They Never Taught You in High School About Going to College*, embody a common theme which Mark highlights in his latest book, and that is the importance of listening. Mark leverages the people he surrounds himself with each and every day. His ability to crowdsource Gen Zers and listen to them as a professor and marketer, creates authentic and genuine advice that will benefit all who read *Decoding Gen Z: 101 Lessons Generation Z Will Teach Corporate America, Marketers & Media.*

Gen Z is more likely to listen to and collaborate with to those they can trust and empathize with. Lesson #13: Give Me A Mentor Not A Manager, highlights the importance Gen Z places on mentorship. Like other Gen Zers, I believe having a mentor allows us to be comfortable communicating with our peers and colleagues, more eager to ask questions, and less apprehensive when it comes to making changes or taking risks in our future careers. Mentorship is a mutually beneficial relationship as Mark demonstrates in his classroom and through his books. It is evident that no matter the age or experience, there is so much to learn from one another.

Generation Z is a generation characterized by flexibility and spontaneity. Smartphones grant us access to everything we could ever need instantaneously, allowing us to make plans in the palm of our hand. We love the idea of spontaneous decisions, having a flexible job that complements this kind of lifestyle is a main priority for Gen Zers. Lesson 94: We Plan for Spontaneity, captures the impromptu decisions Gen Zers make every day.

Gen Z craves travel and adventure. We travel to experience, to be inspired, to gain perspective, and indulge in new cultures. This past semester I was fortunate enough to study abroad in beautiful Barcelona, Spain. During my four months in Europe, I was able to visit five countries and over 15 different cities. More and more Gen Zers are studying abroad each year as we realize the opportunity to learn in a different part of the world is incomparable to the content in a textbook. Other generations criticize Gen Z for our flexible schedules, or our ability to work from home. Laziness is often associated with our work ethic. Yet, I believe Gen Z focuses on maximizing each and every day. We work hard, but we find time to socialize and have fun. We are the generation that has found the perfect balance between work and social life.

Lastly, don't be intimated by our tech savviness, our social fluency or our unique language which Mark features in the Gen Z Glossary in this book. We are delivering a new culture of technology and content that we are introducing to the world and the workplace, creating more efficiency to communicate with each other seamlessly and solve challenges, whether business or social.

So, try not to get to triggered, because this book is low-key and is going to spill the tea on the dope things Gen Z is about to introduce to corporate America, marketers and media. As Lesson #101 states: "We Will Change The World."

Note: If you didn't understand that last paragraph, please refer to the Gen Z Glossary in this book and start to become fluent in our Gen Z language.

INTRODUCTION

Marketers, media and employers – are you fluent in Gen Z?

Do you know how to translate Gen Z terms such as Spill the Tea, Peep My Tweet, Gassing You Up and Drop a Pin?

Are you familiar with some of Gen Z's favorite apps and technology – Forest, Telegram, DePop, Citizen, Facetune and VSCO?

If not, this book, which was written in collaboration with more than 50 Gen Zers ranging from high school freshman to recent college graduates, ages 13 to 23, is intended to help and prepare you for Generation Z which comprises approximately 65 million individuals in the United States. From Havre de Grace, Maryland to Oxford, Mississippi to Los Angeles, California, I interviewed Gen Zers across the nation by text, email, phone, FaceTime and face-to-face.

My interviews with Gen Zers consistently reinforced that they are digital natives, tech-smart, entrepreneurial-spirited, community-minded, socially conscious and purpose-driven, and they prioritize speed, immediacy and efficiency.

Born beginning in the mid-1990s through the early 2010s, the oldest members of Generation Z have recently graduated college and have joined the workforce while other Gen Zers are dispersed across college campuses and high school hallways throughout the nation and around the world experiencing internships and part-time jobs, and the youngest members of Gen Z just graduated kindergarten.

Fittingly, Gen Zers were born during the same period as some of their favorite brands – Amazon (1994), Google (1998), Netflix (1997), iTunes (2003), YouTube (2005), Spotify (2006), Twitter (2006), Venmo (2009), Uber (2009), Instagram (2010) and Snapchat (2011).

Having served as a brand marketer for more than 25 years, I now have the privilege of interacting with hundreds of Gen Zers on a daily basis at two universities. Aside from teaching Gen Zers in marketing and public relations courses at Rutgers University and Montclair State University, I collaborate regularly with them on planning their journey from college to a career. I work one-on-one with Gen Zers in developing their resumes, evolving their professional network, preparing for informational and formal interviews and securing internships and full-time jobs.

In return, Gen Z nation shares with me insights regarding trending topics, media consumption, social media rituals, content likes and dislikes, favorite apps and technologies, concerns and causes and what they are looking for from brand marketers and future employers.

By 2020, Gen Z will account for 40 percent of all consumers according to a 2017 Accenture Report, and some estimate their current spending power to be anywhere from $40 to $140 billion depending on which report you read.

In my attempt to prepare corporate America (employers), brand marketers (brands and agencies), and media (content producers and distributors) for this powerful generation of consumers, I immersed myself in the Gen Z mindset in two ways. First, I reviewed any surveys, studies and insights regarding Gen Z that were recently published, and I conducted extensive one-one meetings, interviews and exchanges with Gen Zers across the nation to validate the research and provide anecdotal commentary which is featured throughout this book.

The result of my research and interactions with Gen Zers is this book which is comprised of 101 pithy lessons Gen Z wanted to share. The lessons provide insights into topics ranging from Gen Z's social media habits and the types of content they produce and consume to how they want brands and marketers to engage them and what they are looking for with respect to culture and mentorship when it comes to internships and jobs.

The book begins with a fun, Gen Z Glossary. I quickly learned that this generation has their own language and lexicon. Every term was provided to me by Gen Zers during our conversations. I intentionally did not Google any terms as I wanted this Gen Z vocabulary to come directly from the mouths and text messages of Gen Zers. Once you review the glossary, you will be able to interpret Spill the Tea, Peep My Tweet, Gassing You Up and Drop a Pin and start to become fluent in Gen Z

I have authored two previous books – *101 Lessons They Never Taught You In College* and *101 Lessons They Never Taught You In High School About Going To College.* I am more excited about this book, *Decoding Gen Z: 101 Lessons Generation Z Will Teach Corporate America, Marketers and Media*, because it goes well beyond a small sample of the population.

My first book was written to help college students prepare for the transition from college to a career, and my second book was written in my attempt to help high school graduates make the seamless transition to college.

This book was written in collaboration with Gen Zers to inform and inspire many audiences including, but not limited to, every employer across the nation who will hire a college graduate or a college intern over the next decade; every brand or organization that is marketing a product, service, cause or philosophy to all consumers born starting in the mid-1990s; every individual who works for an advertising, marketing, promotions, public relations, event, social, digital and shopper marketing consultancy and agency looking to engage Gen Zers on behalf of their clients; and every media company, big or small, that is producing and distributing content with the goal of creating meaningful engagement with Gen Zers. If you belong to any of these organizations, the Gen Z-contributed lessons in this book will be highly relevant and applicable for the work you are doing today and for many years to come.

I am equally excited about this book because I have Gen Zers across the nation who are eager, ready and willing to join me in bringing the book to life via a series of "Z Talks" to companies, organizations and associations where they will deliver real-time Gen Z information and insights that can inform your next campaign, content production or workplace culture initiative.

PART I

GEN Z GLOSSARY

Adulting: Having to take on adult responsibilities

Banger: A great party

Bangin: Usually said as "That's Bangin" or "Banging," meaning super good

Basic: A person who gives into trends and has no originality

Bible: I swear, or I promise

Bit: Discussing your personal bitmoji or someone else's bitmoji

Boujee/Bougie: Someone who has distinctive tastes, extravagant

Clout: Defines your level of coolness

Dead: Finding something extremely hilarious

Deep In The Cut: Far away

Dope: Very cool

Drag: Roasting someone via clever insults

Draking: Feeling emotional, sad

Drop A Pin: Sharing your current location with someone via text

Extra: Someone who is considered high maintenance, has a strong personality, tries too hard

Extreme Ghosting: Aside from not responding to text messages, a person blocks someone else from accessing their social media and blocks their incoming phone calls

Fact/Facts: Agreeing with a statement

Finesse/Finessed: Doing something in a slick way, with ease

Finsta: A fake Instagram account

Fire: Anything that looks good, sounds good, is good

Flame: To roast or make fun of another person

From The Jump: From the beginning

Gassing You Up: Schmoozing someone up or complimenting someone

Go Ahead: Go for it, offering support to a friend

GOAT: Greatest of all-time

Ghosting: One person intentionally stops responding to another person's text

Glow Up/Glowing Up: Someone who has gone through an incredible transformation

Gucci: Good

Highkey: Something that is so obvious to everyone and does not require explanation

HMU: Hit me up, inviting someone to contact you

Hype: Really excited

Hype Up: To give a compliment/overly compliment

Iconic: Something that is memorable

I'm Crying: Hysterically laughing

I'm Done: You have nothing else to say or comment

In My Bag: Feeling emotional

Instafamous: Getting an exceedingly high number of likes on Instagram without having celebrity status

Instagramable: An image or video that is worth putting on your Instagram channel

It's A Dub: Someone who you don't believe is worth your time

L: A losing situation

Left On Read: Somebody who is not replying to your text message

Lit: Something or someone that you think is awesome, cool, amazing

LMR: Asking someone to go to Instagram and like the recent image you posted

Lowkey: Something that is under rated or not talked about

Mood: Agreeing with someone's actions, feelings or plan

Move: It's what's going on or what's happening (see The Wave)

NP: No problem

Nugget: Anything that is adorable

OD: You are doing too much

Peep: To check-out/to look at

Peep My Tweet: Asking someone to go to your Twitter account and favorite your tweet

Piping Hot Tea: Really big gossip

Quality: Complimenting something that is good

Respect: A response to someone who has done something that you think is impressive

Salty: Mad, jealous, angry, upset

Shots Fired: When someone makes a comment/joke at another person

Sliding Into Someone's DM: Direct message someone via Instagram/Twitter you want to meet

SMH: Shaking My Head when disappointed or embarrassed

Snack: A term describing someone who you find attractive

Snap Strike: When you delete Snapchat from your phone but don't delete your account

Spill the Tea: Hot gossip or information to share

Streak: A consecutive streak on Snapchat in which two people snap each other daily

SUP: "What's Up?"

Sus: A sketchy person who shouldn't be trusted

TFW: That Feeling When…

The Wave: It's what's going on or what's happening (a big event or party)

Thirsty: Someone who is desperate for attention and trying too hard

Thread: On Twitter, a person tells a story through a series of tweets

Triggered: To get annoyed, offended by someone else's actions

Thriving: Living your best life

To Ship (someone/something): When you see people who look good together, you "ship" their relationship

Trill: A person who is considered genuine or real

Unsult: A backhanded compliment

V: A substitute for "very," putting more emphasis and intensity on something

Vibe: Good energy

WOAT: Worst of all-time

Woke: Being aware of current events and issues

Wyling: That's crazy

PART II

LOWKEY/HIGHKEY
MOODS OF GEN Z

LESSON 1

WE HAVE OUR OWN GEN Z LANGUAGE

Salty, Nugget, Piping Hot Tea, Sus, Lowkey - Gen Z has their own dialect and if you want to communicate with them, you need to become fluent. All you need to do is refer to the Gen Z glossary of terms at the beginning of this book to start learning their language. "Being on social media since we were young has led to a whole new language that we use primarily because social media platforms like Snapchat, Instagram and Twitter lend themselves to new terms and expressions," said Zoe, Butchen, a member of the University of Connecticut class of 2022. "While older generations may feel a bit disconnected by our language, it's kind of cool to talk in our Gen Z language and have other generations try to interpret what we are saying."

LESSON 2

WE WANT TO PERSONALIZE OUR PURCHASES, MEDIA & RESPONSIBILITIES

From pursuing their passions and starting new clubs in high school to designing customized courses in college, Gen Z has grown up in a world where they have personalized just about everything. In a Google report, 26% of Gen Zers expect retailers to offer a more personalized shopping experience based on past shopping habits.[1] The *Harvard Business Review* writes, "We live in an increasingly personalized society. We choose individualized playlists instead of radio stations. We self-select our news sources and our TV shows... Everything is geared, just for us."[2] No generation embodies personalization more than Gen Z. For corporate America, this presents a first-of-its-kind opportunity to transform the traditional assigning of work tasks to junior level executives to more of a collaborative process with members of Gen Z as they join the workforce in co-designing their job responsibilities in a way that is empowering and fulfilling. For brand marketers, look no further for inspiration and proof-of-concept than the century-old Converse brand where, "customers can design their own sneakers from scratch, starting with the color of the rubber and finishing with the eyelets and laces."[3] Alexa Restaino, a communications major in the Rutgers University class

1. Sehl, K. (2018, April 20). Generation Z: Everything Social Marketers Need to Know. Retrieved from https://blog.hootsuite.com/generation-z-statistics-social-marketers/
2. Bapat, V. (2018, May 21). Why You Should Let Employees Personalize Their Job Descriptions. Retrieved from https://hbr.org/2018/05/why-you-should-let-employees-personalize-their-job-descriptions
3. Milnes, H., Flynn, K., Liffreing, I., Bhattacharyya, S., & Pathak, S. (2016, February 19). Behind the scenes at Converse's in-store 'Blank Canvas' customization shop. Retrieved from https://digiday.com/marketing/behind-scenes-converses-store-blank-canvas-customization-shop/

of 2019, commented, "From customizing my own music playlist for every mood I am feeling to designing my own sneakers to personalizing my watches, marketers who will successfully engage with Gen Z will offer options for us to customize and personalize their products and services."

LESSON 3

FACEBOOK HAS NO FUTURE WITH GEN Z

In a Gen Z survey by Montclair University's student-run agency, Hawk Communications, when asked which one social media channel they prefer over all others, Facebook was a distant fifth at only 7% compared to Facebook-owned Instagram (45%), Twitter and Snapchat.[4] This was also the case with a Piper Jaffray survey from 2017 where only 9% of teens selected Facebook as their favorite platform a decline of 4% from 2016, compared to Snapchat (47%).[5] In the Hawk Communications survey, when asked why they use Facebook, the majority (81%) said to follow family and friends. "I use Facebook to stay connected with an older audience, such as family and other adults. Other than that, I have a preference for using Instagram, Twitter and Snapchat for most of my social media usage," commented Amanda Peacock, a member of the Montclair State University class of 2021. "I think Facebook will be near extinction by the time the youngest Gen Zers are in college as it is primarily being used by our parents, while we are communicating with Snapchat and Instagram," added Carly Galasso, a 2018 graduate of Rutgers University. "Our generation just doesn't use Facebook. It really is the social media platform of choice for older people," said Amanda Romano, a member of the Rutgers University class of 2019. Among the more than 50 Gen Zers I interviewed for this book, these were the only three Gen Zers who even referenced Facebook when discussing their social media consumption.

4. Hawk Communications, Montclair State University, Generation Z Survey conducted online via Google, April-June, 2018

5. Abadi, M. (2018, January 19). Millennials have taken down dozens of industries - but it looks like Gen Z will be the ones to hurt Facebook. Retrieved from http://www.businessinsider.com/generation-z-facebook-2018-1

LESSON 4

BRANDS SHOULD HAVE A PURPOSE BEYOND THE TRANSACTION

Beware brands... Gen Z is looking for you to have a higher purpose that goes well beyond a simple transaction. A recent Wharton Business School study found that Millennials and Gen Z are, "mainly interested in supporting brands that are ethical, caring and strive to do the right thing."[6] "Brands need to stand for something that is not only important in today's culture and society if they want to have a long-term relationship with Gen Z, but the brand's purpose must be sharable with our way of living," said Stephanie Michael, a member of the Montclair State University of 2019. "And, don't try to fool us, because we can see right through inauthentic marketing. We will take the time necessary to review your past posts, tweets and other content and call you out for misleading our generation." In a CNBC feature on Gen Z and what they are seeking from brands, they wrote, "Faith in companies is a big issue for this group (Gen Z), with 43 percent trusting long-established brands. But corporates better tread carefully, according to one respondent. 'Nobody's going to buy a product from a corporation who you know is just out for the money, unless you see them doing good stuff.'"[7] Before marketing to Gen Z, brand marketers should take quality time to listen to Gen Zers and understand what causes are most important and determine how they can authentically align with their

---

6. Selko, A. (2018, July 12). Top 10 Brands Millennials, Gen Z Trust. Retrieved from http://www.industryweek.com/companies-executives/top-10-brands-millennials-gen-z-trust

7. Handley, L. (2018, April 16). There's a generation below millennials and here's what they want from brands. Retrieved from https://www.cnbc.com/2018/04/09/generation-z-what-they-want-from-brands-and-businesses.html

brand. "This is more than corporate social responsibility and do-
nating money to charity," says Mark Bonchek, founder of Shift
Thinking. "It's finding the deeper meaning of what you do every
day. Go beyond doing something *to* or *for* your customer and create a shared purpose *with* them." Even at the workplace, Gen Zers
are looking for employers who have a purpose beyond generating
revenue. "Many of us value working one day for a company that
serves a higher purpose, positively impacting causes and issues
that are important to Gen Z," said Shelby Fong, a member of the
Rutgers University class of 2019. "In speaking to other Gen Zers,
I learned that they are narrowing down their employer of choice
to companies that give back to their community and the world."

LESSON 5

WE ENJOY A DIGITAL DETOX

According to a survey of more than 1,000 Gen Zers by Origin, the in-house research division of advertising agency, Hill Holliday, 34% said they are permanently quitting social media and 64% percent plan to take a break as social media causes a wide range of emotions.[8] Alexa Restaino a communications major in the Rutgers University class of 2019, said that she and her Gen Z friends regularly do a digital detox or cleanse and simply take a vacation from their social media channels. "While we don't delete our accounts, my group of friends will make a commitment several times a year to shut down social media for one week at a time. We typically turn off Snapchat and Instagram as those are our most active channels and we get back to face-to-face communication and experiencing life first-hand." Christina Hamdan, a member of the University of Delaware class of 2019, commented, "I am currently on a vacation from my social media that has already lasted a month. I am taking a break because I was posting content that I thought my followers wanted to see, but it wasn't really an accurate portrayal of me. My social media vacation has allowed me to experience life to the fullest." For marketers, there is an opportunity to offer alternative experiences and engagement opportunities knowing that Gen Z is shutting down their social media for a day, week or even a month. As social media continues to increase in popularity, the Gen Zers I interviewed believe that shutting down social media for periods of time will become equally as popular.

---

8. McAteer, O. (2018, March 09). Gen Z is quitting social media in droves because it makes them unhappy, study finds. Retrieved from https://www.campaignlive.com/article/gen-z-quitting-social-media-droves-makes-unhappy-study-finds/1459007

LESSON 6

MAKE YOUR PRODUCTS & PLACES INSTAGRAMABLE

❝ We are constantly in the mindset of shooting and sharing the perfect photo," said Stephanie Michael, a class of 2019 Montclair State University student. "We obsess over how the images we share on Instagram and our other social media channels are not only going to look, but how well they are going to be received by our followers." When it comes to brands and their retail locations – restaurants, stores, shops – if the brand doesn't offer an Instagramable, visually appealing backdrop, they have just lost an opportunity for Gen Z's advocacy. "Instagram is a place to glorify your life experience. These pictures last forever and are seen by hundreds or thousands of followers. Even if you can delete them, they're prone to screenshots from your followers. So, users make sure that their feeds are consistent with the image they want to publicize to the world."[9] Sally Meli, a 2017 graduate of Wagner College added, "Instagram now has a "save" feature where you can save any other account's post to an album onto your account without anyone else knowing you've saved it. When I am looking for new restaurants to try with friends, I will go into my saved food folder on Instagram to look at photos of food and restaurants that other people have shared. A lot of the time, we pick a restaurant or dish to try based on how it looks on Instagram."

---

9. Pendse, V. (2017, November 09). Instagram and Snapchat: The Tale of the Gen Z Tape. Retrieved from https://www.adweek.com/digital/vandita-pendse-blend-guest-post-instagram-vs-snapchat/

LESSON 7

ADVERTISING IS A TURN OFF

As the most popular social media platforms for Gen Z, Instagram and Snapchat, focus on driving incremental revenue, they are turning off some of their most valuable users. Ad Age wrote, "It makes sense that 69% of Gen Z already avoids ads," in referencing a Kantar Millward Brown study of Gen Zers[10]. "We are not at a tipping point yet, but there is a growing dislike by Gen Zers when it comes to the blatant advertising on our favorite social media channels," said Sabrina Araullo, a member of the Montclair State University class of 2018. "Brand marketers should focus more on how to customize their paid or sponsored content specifically for a channel like Instagram or Snapchat so that it naturally and authentically integrates into my feed and I am more likely to engage with it. Today, too many brands are taking a screaming commercial approach and that will backfire with our generation." Additionally, while advertising and marketing to Gen Z, "do not attempt to emulate their humor as it will most likely miss the mark and have a negative impact," said Rachel Boyce, a member of the Stockton University class of 2018.

---

10. Innes., C., & Innes, C. (2017, May 23). Gen Z Hates Your Ads ... but They Love Your Videos. Retrieved from http://adage.com/article/agency-viewpoint/gen-z-hates-ads-love-videos/309105/

LESSON 8

NETFLIX IS OUR GO-TO NETWORK

Accordingtoa 2018 survey of Gen Zers by Hawk Communications, the student-run public relations agency at Montclair State University, more than 85% have a subscription to Netflix, more than 50% admit that Netflix is their preferred method of streaming video and 43% prefer Netflix over all other sources including cable and network television for watching video content.[11] A story in HuffPost on the media consumption habits of Gen Z cited a survey which uncovered that 70% of Generation Z watches Netflix each month. The same story referenced the Deloitte Digital Democracy Survey in which 40% of millennials and Gen Zers binge watch on a weekly basis.[12] "Netflix offers instantaneous gratification when it comes to watching original content, movies and television shows," said Sabrina Araullo, a 2018 graduate of Montclair State University. "We can watch an entire series in one sitting at a time convenient for our schedule with no commercial breaks, which is why the majority of GenZers are turning away from traditional television." Media and marketers in other industries should determine how they can apply the "Netflix" model to their business to more effectively engage Gen Z.

11. Hawk Communications, Montclair State University, Generation Z Survey conducted online via Google, April-June, 2018

12. Radcliffe, D. (2017, November 27). The Media Habits Of Millennials, Generation Z, And The Rest Of Us:
In Five Key Charts. Retrieved from https://www.huffingtonpost.co.uk/entry/the-media-habits-of-millennials-generation-z-and-the-rest-of-us-in-five-key-charts_uk_5a149436e4b0815d3ce65ac5?guccounter=1

LESSON 9

WE WANT MORE H.I.

In a multi-generation survey conducted by community technology provider 8 X 8, "results showed that the Gen Z respondents were more likely than either the millennial or the Gen X respondents to report that they value face-to-face communication, with an emphasis on effectiveness over convenience."[13] Contrary to popular opinion, Gen Z does not refrain entirely from human interaction. In fact, they are craving more of what I like to call, H.I. (Human Interaction). "Fifty-three percent of Generation Z said they prefer in-person discussion" at the workplace.[14] All Gen Zers who I interviewed emphasized the need for more face-to-face time at work especially with mentors and colleagues, more time in-person with a network of peers and other individuals who share a common purpose and passion and even more time with companies and brands via unique opportunities and experiences. "The greatest myth about our generation is that our heads are buried in our phones, we can't hold a conversation and we avoid meaningful contact with other people," said Summer Beal, a 2018 graduate of East Stroudsburg University. "There is a reason mentorship is important to us. There is a reason we shut down social media for periods at a time and there is a reason why we are passionate about cause-related movements. We want to collaborate with others face-to-face in a meaningful way to learn, grow and evolve... and in the process, make our communities and world a better place to live."

13. Generation Z Values Face-To-Face Business Communication. (2017, February 28). Retrieved from http://yozell.com/blog/generation-z-values-face-face-business-communication/
14. Patel, D. (2017, September 22). 8 Ways Generation Z Will Differ From Millennials In The Workplace. Retrieved from https://www.forbes.com/sites/deeppatel/2017/09/21/8-ways-generation-z-will-differ-from-millennials-in-the-workplace/#b44b7e876e5e

LESSON 10

COMMUNITIES ARE CRITICALLY IMPORTANT

❝ Whether it's gathering all their mates in a Whatsapp group or it's the 60% who say they share their knowledge online, life's all about building collaborative communities," when it comes to Gen Z.[15] Online, in-person or a hybrid, small communities of like-minded Gen Zers who share a common passion, purpose and interest is increasingly becoming popular. "Communities or networks of people who share common interests whether that be volunteering, food or video games is very important to our generation," commented Jessica Ortega, a member of the Montclair State University class of 2019. "These communities not only feed our passions, they give us balance in our lives, especially when it comes to work life balance. Companies and workplaces should take a page from colleges and universities and offer employees clubs centered around passions and interests or better yet, offer employees the chance to start their own club." Imagine if your company started their own eSports team, dinner club or fitness community. They would become the talk of their industry, and more importantly, resonate more with Gen Zers as they join the workforce over the next decade.

---

15. Evans, D. (2017, November 30). So, Where Does Generation Z Fit into the Workplace? Retrieved from https://medium.com/@daveevansap/so-where-does-generation-z-fit-into-the-workplace-3b3bd279b8c

LESSON 11

FRIENDS & FAMILY INFLUENCE US THE MOST

According to a 2018 survey of Gen Zers by Hawk Communications, the student-run public relations agency at Montclair State University, when it comes to content on social media, friends and family (27%) have the greatest influence on Gen Z more than social media influencers (23%), subject matter experts (14%) and celebrities (12%).[16] In a story regarding the most interesting facts about Gen Z, blogger Dan Schawbel referenced that, "43% said their family influences their purchasing decisions the most followed by friends (35%)".[17] Katelyn Woebse, a member of Hawk Communications commented, "When Gen Zers consider a brand or making a purchase, we conduct extensive research and our friends and family are by far our greatest influence. Social media enables us to crowdsource friends and family about their experience with a certain brand or product to help us gain a better understanding before we invest what limited budget we may have." Brand marketers should take notice as social media influencers, subject matter experts and celebrities may have greater social media reach, but wield less influence than family and friends when it comes to Generation Z.

16. Hawk Communications, Montclair State University, Generation Z Survey conducted online via Google, April-June, 2018

17. Schawbel, D. (2014, July 17). Home. Retrieved from http://danschawbel.com/
blog/39-of-the-most-interesting-facts-about-generation-z/

LESSON 12

WE LOVE STREAKING

❝My longest streak is 660 days and I have as many as 15-20 streaks simultaneously," said Sophia Kazee, a member of the University of Pittsburgh class of 2021. What makes Snapchat so much more addicting is the streak. "I Snapchat a friend consecutively and I want to build Snapchat streaks on my friends list. It's an addictive game of sorts," said Ryan Jannuzzi, Rutgers University class of 2022. "Snapchat has given users a reason to use the app other than for just entertainment. It created the need to maintain a habit, a tradition, a lifestyle. Those with important Snapstreaks to maintain will find a reason to return to the app every single day. The longer the streak, the more it matters to them."[18] "We love streaks, especially with those who we have a special interest in. It shows that we are thinking of the other person and share the same level of dedication to be fully engaged with one another even if we are not always with them," added Rahima Tokhi, Rutgers University class of 2018. "There's nothing more heartbreaking than reaching a long streak and then having it end because you or the other person did not keep up with it. I remember getting into a serious fight with a guy I was dating, and we had a streak that was well over 200 days. We were giving each other the silent treatment at the time and I was waiting for him to possibly snap me back because there's no way he was going to break that, right? I was wrong. Neither he nor I kept the streak going because we were too prideful and then we had to start all over again once we made amends. It was quite sad."

---

18. Snapchat's snapstreaks: The latest millennial craze. (2018, May 14). Retrieved from https://www.mediablazegroup.com/blog/snapchats-snapstreaks/

PART III

SPILLING THE TEA ON GEN Z AT THE WORKPLACE

LESSON 13

GIVE ME A MENTOR NOT A MANAGER

❝ I strongly believe in having mentors, especially in the workplace at an internship or in my first job out of college," said Antonia Attardo, a communications major in the Rutgers University class of 2019. "Finding someone who I can trust to guide me through that first critical year or two out of college is much more important to my long-term career success than an authoritative manager who is focused solely on the day-to-day tactical execution." Antonia is not alone. In a survey of 5,000 Gen Zers from more than 100 colleges by Door of Clubs, "37% of respondents noted health care benefits were the most important benefit, closely followed by a mentorship program (33%)."[19] Mentorship was even more important for Gen Z than time-off and being able to work remotely. A mentorship-driven agenda by Gen Z produces mutually beneficial results for not only the Gen Zer but the company for which they work. The new employee is inspired and empowered, while their company's employee retention rates will most likely see a spike in a positive direction. "Even though members of Generation Z enjoy their independence, they don't have the know-it-all attitude millennials have occasionally been accused of. That means if you offer them opportunities to grow, they'll leap at them. The opportunity to learn from experienced people they respect is one of the most important qualities Gen Z looks for in the type of work they engage in."[20]

19. Clubs, D. O. (2017, November 30). What 5,000 Gen Z'ers Tell Us About the Future of Work. Retrieved from https://medium.com/@doorofclubs/what-5-000-gen-zers-tell-us-about-the-future-of-work-6dd00f796e8f

20. Rampton, J. (2018, May 25). 8 Strategies to Avoid Wasting Your Company's Gen-Z Talent. Retrieved from https://www.entrepreneur.com/article/313769

LESSON 14

WE WANT TO KNOW WHY

While previous generations in their first job out of college may have put their heads down and did what they were asked or told, Gen Z wants to understand the objective in the request and the "why" behind the assignment. "Anyone can accept an assignment, but Gen Z wants to go beyond the tactical instructions and understand the ultimate goal in accomplishing the task," commented Kelsey Geisenheimer, a 2018 graduate of Syracuse University. "Gen Zers are comfortable and confident enough to ask questions that go beyond tactics to answer why we are receiving the specific assignment. We want to better understand the strategy behind the ask." Employers need to prepare themselves for a generation that will challenge them with questions. Gen Z is looking for a role that takes them beyond just being a cog in the machine. "Create a company culture that rewards curiosity and ambition by providing the social rewards, mentorship, and feedback Gen Z craves, along with the transparency and flexibility they and Millennials both cherish."[21]

21. Power, R. (2017, December 04). Millennials Are Old News: What Do Gen Z Workers Want? Retrieved from https://www.inc.com/rhett-power/millennials-are-old-news-what-do-gen-z-workers-want.html

LESSON 15

LIFE WORK BALANCE IS A PRIORITY

"Generation Z…is expected to handle work and life differently than previous generations and to pose growing challenges for employers in the coming years."[22] Previous generations in the past 20 years began to prioritize the concept of "work life balance." Well, for Gen Z, life outside the office, in many cases, is equally as important as work, and a shift is underway from a work life balance to a "life work balance." "Work is a top priority for me especially since I just graduated," said Kelsey Geisenheimer, a member of the Syracuse University class of 2018. "However, a balance of family, friends and social experiences during the work week is what is going to energize and recharge me and allow me to exceed expectations at work. It's important for our generation to work in a culture where we are not expected to be chained to our desk or cubicle and have the opportunity to get out of the office for dinner, happy hour, a concert or go to a museum with friends or mentors knowing we are going to be back at it the next day."

---

22. Brin, D. W. (2014, July 31). Gen Z Could Soon Pose Greater HR Challenges. Retrieved from https://blog.shrm.org/workforce/gen-z-could-soon-pose-greater-hr-challenges

LESSON 16

WE WANT TO SEE THE PROJECT THROUGH COMPLETION

"Please don't invite me just to do the grunt work early on in a project or presentation and then ignore me when it comes time for the big reveal," said Sierra Haney, a 2018 graduate of The College of New Jersey. "If you believe I can deliver value in the first or second phase of program development than offer me the opportunity to be part of the team that is going to see the project through completion. I feel I am as invested as any other co-worker who has contributed to the project and while I may be the most junior, I want to see it through to the completion as much as the most senior executive." In a column in Entrepreneur, John Rampton agreed with Sierra when he wrote, "Unlike traditionalists, this generation isn't motivated by titles or climbing the corporate ladder. That doesn't mean they'll reject leadership -- they would just rather have a stake in a company's growth or success, regardless of what that looks like. One way to achieve this is by allowing your Gen Z employees to have complete ownership of a project they can implement from start to finish. Give them clear expectations and guidelines from the get-go, and watch them take initiative."[23]

---

23. Rampton, J. (2018, May 25). 8 Strategies to Avoid Wasting Your Company's Gen-Z Talent. Retrieved from https://www.entrepreneur.com/article/313769

LESSON 17

CULTURE IS CRITICALLY IMPORTANT

In a column in Inc. featuring what Gen Z seeks at the workplace, Rhett Power wrote, "Successful organizations today are not only building this rewarding culture, but upholding it as a key identifier for their brands. For example, the media intelligence company Meltwater designed its culture around building and reinforcing an entrepreneurial spirit in its people. This culture, represented by MER - which stands for Moro, Enere, and Respekt -- is the Norwegian word for "more," and it helps the company celebrate achievements without losing the passion to succeed."[24] Even more than salary, benefits and vacation days, workplace culture is critically important to Gen Zers. "Based on my internships throughout college, I came to realize that the culture of a company or organization for me and many other recent graduates is perhaps the most critical component in what I am looking for in my first job, and more importantly, why I will stay or leave that job," commented Sabrina Araullo, Montclair State University, class of 2018. "A large chunk of my life is going to be dedicated to my job and my employer, and I want to be passionate not only about the work I produce but the company I produce it for." For her agency's blog, Caroline Jacoby of Adrenaline wrote about Gen Z's forthcoming influence on corporate culture, "The disruption that Millennials caused in the past two decades was largely born of innovation and technology. The coming disruption from Gen Z will be revolutionary from a cultural standpoint.

24. Power, R. (2017, December 04). Millennials Are Old News: What Do Gen Z Workers Want? Retrieved from https://www.inc.
   com/rhett-power/millennials-are-old-news-what-do-gen-z-workers-want.html

For brands to be successful, they'll have to understand cultural intersectionality over generational silo."[25] "Yes, salary is important, but Gen Zers value the workplace culture even more," added Shelby Fong, a member of the Rutgers University class of 2019. "If a company does not have a collaborative culture and work environment, it will significantly reduce their chances of attracting top Gen Z talent."

25. GEN Z: CULTURE BUILDERS. (n.d.). Retrieved from http://www.adrenalineagency.com/blog/gen-z-culture-builders/

LESSON 18

WE'RE NOT WORKING NINE TO FIVE

Gen Zers look at their world through a 24-hour, seven day-a-week lense. The nine to five mindset of previous generations is officially extinct... at least for many Gen Zers. "With over 75% of the workforce set to be made up of Millennials by 2025 it is predicted that by 2030 the traditional 9 to 5 working day will no longer exist. The change is taking place because the Millennial and Generation Z workforce are one that are constantly digitally connected enabling them to work in complete different ways to those from the Baby Boomer generation."[26] When discussing the workplace and jobs with Gen Z, very few advocated for the traditional nine to five. "As we live our lives in more of a 24/7 tech world, the nine to five mentality just doesn't exist with our generation," said Jessica Ortega, a member of the Montclair State University class of 2019. "As we consider internships and jobs, we are looking for flexibility as it relates to when we arrive at work and when we depart as well as where we conduct our work. With today's technology we can be highly effective and efficient anytime and anywhere."

26. Faulkner, R. (2018, April 12). Millennials and Gen Z: Driving the death of the 9 to 5? Retrieved from https://www.replgroup.com/millennials-genz-death-9-5/

LESSON 19

WE USE TECHNOLOGY
TO OUR ADVANTAGE

As someone who teaches more than 125 Gen Zers every semester at Rutgers University and Montclair State University, I can attest to the fact that this generation quickly adopts technology that makes completing assignments, especially group projects, highly efficient. "It's just part of our lifestyle to adopt technology that allows us to collaborate anywhere, anytime efficiently. There is not enough time in our day to be inefficient," said Katelyn Woebse, member of the Montclair State University class of 2020. "It's second nature for us in college to quickly adopt tools and technology like Google Drive, GroupMe and Slack if it is going to make completing an assignment more effective especially as the college experience becomes more virtual and members of a group may actually only see each other face-to-face once a week," said Quinn Heinrich, a 2018 graduate of Loyola Marymount University. "As we enter the workforce, we are bringing these tools and technology with us and we won't hesitate to recommend anything that helps get the job completed more efficiently especially if we work with teams that span multiple time zones." Corporate America should be listening to Gen Z as they enter the workforce. They will be arriving with solid recommendations and tech-based solutions regarding how to conduct business in new and innovative ways and corporations and organizations should not resist.

LESSON 20

WORKING FROM HOME WORKS WELL

While older generations have no problem with commuting by planes, trains, automobiles and busses for hours a day, each way, especially in major cities, Gen Z considers it a complete waste of time. "We are wasting our time and the company's time commuting five days a week," said Quinn Heinrich, a 2018 graduate of Loyola Marymount University. "One or more days a week I can be highly productive from my happy place. It offers me the flexibility to jump on assignments much earlier in the morning before I normally would arrive at the office, and by doing that, I can also carve out some time during the day for a workout or a lunch social and I return to my assignments more energized, excited and focused to meet my deadlines." It's a simple and smart concept – instead of sitting in a car, bus or train for as many as one to two hours commuting to work in the morning and one to two more hours in the evening, Gen Zers will maximize those hours from their home and be well ahead of their assignments and deliverables by the time most of their colleagues are just arriving at the office.

LESSON 21

DESIGN OFFICES TO MAKE THEM GEN Z FRIENDLY

❝ Both Millennials and Gen Z, though different generations, do share their love for a great workplace. Such offices can be driven by a mélange of emerging trends and the desire to provide something extra, more than just being a physical space. As these generations will continue to thrive, designers can ideate with employers and employees to create a design that will be more radical, adaptable and balanced."[27] Corporate America: Continue to tear down your private offices with doors and wasted space, open up your work workspace, do away with assigned seating, create collaboration centers, have the most senior executives sit alongside the most junior employees, bolster your technology, throw out the old furniture and invest in ergonomic desks and chairs, add in some happy hour time, provide employees the opportunity to bring their pets to work, install a few nap pods and cater unlimited snacks and beverages because if you are going to attract the top talent from the next generation entering the workforce, that is exactly what Gen Z is looking for. "I have interned for companies with Gen Z designed offices and the employee morale is better, the enthusiasm is improved and creative problem solving is enhanced," said Quinn Heinrich, a 2018 graduate of Loyola Marymount University. "The traditional, stuffy corporate offices should be a thing of the past and it should give way to a workplace environment that allows for maximum collaboration and relationship building."

---

27. Thacker, I. (2018, May 11). Rethinking Workplace Design for Millennials and Gen Z. Retrieved from https://www.entrepreneur.com/article/313295

LESSON 22

WE WANT TO CONTINUE TO LEARN

Saddled by tuition debt, Gen Z does not fear education. In fact, they have a desire to learn more and evolve professionally and socially. Social media strategy company, Bazaarvoice, in a story regarding Gen Zers and what they are looking for when it comes to employment recommended to employers, "offer chances for autonomy, personal growth, and continued education to appeal to this incredibly motivated group."[28] Gen Z lives by the expression, "be a student for life." However, they are hoping corporate America can support their desire to learn. "Gen Z wants to work for companies that recognize that continuing our education allows us to deliver greater value at work," said Quinn Heinrich, a 2018 graduate of Loyola Marymount University. "Ideally, we want to be employed by companies that offer mini scholarships, grants or tuition assistance to go back to school for an MBA or graduate degree, a certificate program or just the opportunity to attend a conference or training session and in return, we deliver those learnings back to our colleagues, teams and clients." Carly Galasso, a 2018 graduate of Rutgers University, added, "Advanced degrees and continuing to educate ourselves will become increasingly more important for my generation as we join the workforce."

---

28. Huber, L. (2018, February 21). Sneak peek at what Gen Z wants from employers. Retrieved from https://theamericangenius.com/business-news/sneak-peek-gen-z-wants-employers/

LESSON 23

EMBRACE OUR ENTREPRENEURIAL SPRIT

" According to a recent study by Northeastern University, as a group, Gen Z tends to be 'highly self-directed, demonstrated by a strong desire to work for themselves, study entrepreneurship, and design their own programs of study in college'."[29] Brand marketers and employers should recognize and embrace the entrepreneurial spirit of Gen Z. "We are prosumers...we are consumers as much as any other generation before us, but we leverage technology and social media to produce, market and sell products as well," said Katelyn Woebse, a member of the Montclair University class of 2020. "If I am a consumer brand or even an employer, I would create an incubator comprised of Gen Zers and have them utilize apps like Poshmark that are easy to navigate and let them realize the full potential of their entrepreneurial spirit." One company has already adopted this approach. Kidbox, the children's clothing company, created a Kid's Board of Directors which is comprised exclusively of Gen Zers, age 12 or younger. Other brands or employers that take this innovative step could be at the forefront of a new business unit and revenue stream.

29. Shear, L. (n.d.). With eyes wide open, Generation Z looks to serve, share, and impact | Relate by Zendesk. Retrieved from https:// relate.zendesk.com/articles/eyes-wide-open-generation-z-looks-serve-share-impact/

LESSON 24

WE CAN TEACH OLDER GENERATIONS A FEW LESSONS

With Gen Z's rapid adoption of technology and the evolution of popular social media channels including Snapchat and Instagram, Gen Z can teach older generations a few things during their next internship or that first full-time job after college. "Members of Generation Z have not known a world without smartphones or social media. Think about it: The iPhone was released in 2007, when the oldest members of the generation were only 11-years-old and the youngest had yet to be born. Technology is all they have known, and their technological abilities are almost second nature," writes James Clark in Entrepreneur for a story about Gen Zers entering the workforce.[30] "We are so confident that we are more fluent in social media than any other generation and we adopt and utilize technology so rapidly, that I believe that a major shift will occur at the workplace as more and more Gen Zers join the workforce over the next five to 10 years," said Katelyn Woebse, a member of the class of 2020 at Montclair State University. "Instead of only learning in that first job, we believe we will actually be teaching senior managers and colleagues valuable lessons and insights when it comes to technology, content and social and digital media in a way that delivers value and drives business impact." Instead of ignoring the new kid on the block, corporate America would be wise to proactively solicit their counsel and advice when it comes

---

30. Clark, J. (2017, August 07). Generation Z: Are We Ready for the New Workforce? Retrieved from https://www.entrepreneur.com/article/296262

to topics where Gen Z brings a greater fluency. Brand marketers should do the same and create proprietary panels of Gen Zers for everything from developing products to testing new advertising and marketing.

LESSON 25

MAKE ROOM FOR MY PASSIONS

Pursuing their passions is a priority for Gen Z, writes Larry Alton in Inc.[31] Lynda Spiegel added, "Gen Z seems to have benefited from great economic and cultural timing, affording them the opportunity to truly follow their passions. Older generations have traditionally had to wait until retirement to find work that holds meaning…but Gen Z, with its collective drive and ability, doesn't need to wait."[32] Being an accountant, analyst, or advertising executive may be what Gen Z does, but it does not define who they are. To truly learn who Gen Z is, you need to invest some time with them and understand their personal passions and if you are corporate America, you need to make room for those passions if you want to retain the talented individuals who comprise Generation Z. "My ultimate goal is to be able to work in a field that I'm passionate about, and when people give you the space to be creative and think outside of the box, you're more likely to invest your time and effort into something you truly care about," said Alyssa Rivers, a member of the Rutgers University class of 2020. "In the workplace, there needs to be room to foster new ideas, growth, and encouragement for people to pursue their passions, so they can contribute without worry of consequences." The workplace can and should be a venue for Gen Z to immerse themselves in their work AND their passions.

31. Alton, L. (2018, March 14). Why Millennials and Gen Z are Going to Take the Small Business World by Storm. Retrieved from https://www.inc.com/larry-alton/why-millennials-gen-z-are-going-to-take-small-business-world-by-storm.html

32. For Generation Z, Passion is the Future of Work. (2015, June 5). Retrieved from https://www.cornerstoneondemand.com/rework/generation-z-passion-future-work

LESSON 26

SHARING IS SMART

❝ Gen Zers have grown up using shared drive technology and look to collaborate in the most efficient manner. Corporations should evaluate how to best utilize sharing platforms to avoid the back and forth of emailed drafts," said Cole Butchen, Cornell University class of 2019. "It may not be Google. It may not even exist yet, but brands and companies should be researching how to develop a sharing platform that is more effective than Google Drive." The N-Gen blog summarized it well when discussing Gen Z, technology and the workplace, "The goal is to leverage technology so that new (Gen Z) recruits perceive your organization as modern and tech-savvy, as well as ensuring the technology you use enhances communication and efficiency."[33]

33. How Gen Z Uses Technology. (2017, November 16). Retrieved from http://www.ngenperformance.com/blog/gen-z-2/how-gen-z-uses-technology

LESSON 27

MAKE LARGE COMPANIES MORE PERSONAL

As Gen Zers enter the workforce, they are looking for large corporations with thousands of employees to offer them a more personal experience. "Ways to get involved, such as clubs and interest groups, is something that Gen Zers look for as they search for internships and full-time opportunities," said Cole Butchen, Cornell University class of 2019. "At work, we want to connect with colleagues beyond a specific assignment or one-off project. Large corporations can benefit from having communities that foster real connections and shared passions. Through smaller interest groups, we gain a greater sense of belonging and commitment." It may be easier said than done, but making large companies smaller and more personal, is very important to Gen Zers.

LESSON 28

LET'S DO LUNCH

"Lunchtime is our escape from the office," said Brooke Stern, a member of the Cornell University class of 2019. "I need to give my mind a break to give my best. Gen Z would prefer to have the chance to get out of the office and enjoy a new environment where other generations routinely eat right at their desks and plow through their work." It sounds simple enough, but whether it is lunch, an off-site networking opportunity or a social event, Gen Z is looking to stretch their legs, leave the office to recharge their batteries and their brains and return with greater energy and enthusiasm, so give them that opportunity daily. "Lunch and other opportunities for breaks not only offers the chance to clear our minds, but also presents an opportunity to meet someone new and evolve our network," commented Paige Daly, a member of the University of New Haven class of 2020.

LESSON 29

WE WANT TO KNOW WHERE WE STAND

"At the workplace, we want to know exactly where we stand. We yearn for jobs where there are formal reviews and informal monthly or quarterly check-ins regarding our performance and short-term and long-term career goals," said Quinn Heinrich, a 2018 graduate of Loyola Marymount University. Gen Z not only wants to be held accountable, but they want to collaborate with employers on all aspects of their career progress and evolution. They are looking for transparency and straight talk with respect to advancement and opportunity. If they work for a company or organization that is not providing it, they will have no regrets in seeking one that will. "Gen Zers want to receive ongoing constructive feedback as we have a desire to improve and evolve. The last thing we want to learn after the fact is that we could have executed something differently or better earlier in the assignment process," said Shelby Fong, a member of the Rutgers University class of 2019. "Career development and growth opportunities are very important to our generation and early and consistent feedback will help us get there."

LESSON 30

PLEASE DON'T WASTE OUR TIME

Gen Z values efficiency, immediacy and continuous productivity so don't waste their time at work. Other generations may have gotten away with calling a meeting for 10:00 a.m. and then strolling in at 10:15 a.m. and wasting 15 minutes of everyone's time in the room. Gen Z regards that as counterproductive. "We value every minute of every day especially when it comes to work and delivering our assignments on time," said Melissa Jannuzzi, a 2017 graduate of Rutgers University. "We prioritize efficiency especially when it comes to meetings knowing if we can gain back some time as a result of an efficiently led meeting, we can invest that time into the priorities of the day." Managers and supervisors - start your meetings right on time or even a minute early, and more importantly, set a detailed agenda and distribute prior to the meeting. That type of proactive approach can turn a scheduled 60-minute meeting into one that lasts 45 minutes and gives back 15 minutes to your Gen Z colleagues, something they will greatly value and appreciate.

LESSON 31

FLEX TIME IS OUR KIND OF TIME

As the first Gen Zers graduate college and secure employment, corporate America needs to prepare themselves for a generation that is looking to work by a new set of rules. "When searching for jobs, we are looking for companies that offer flexibility when it comes to where they allow us to work and at what hours," said Austin Sommerer, a 2017 graduate of Penn State University. "In our tech-centric way of working and living, we realize that our work will surround us 24/7, so we are seeking employers who have future-forward mindsets and offer the opportunity to work remotely and even non-traditional hours."

LESSON 32

WE EMBRACE DIVERSE COLLABORATION

"Gen Z workers are looking for a workplace with values similar to their own. And, as the most racially diverse generation in America, they need a workplace that prioritizes diversity just as much as they do."[34] "Collaboration with a diverse group of people, experiences and mindsets is very important to us," said Ryan Stiesi, a member of the Rutgers University class of 2019. "If there are two companies or brands from two different industries looking to market and engage Gen Z, they should explore an innovative way to come together and combine forces on a campaign, initiative or even a product around a social issue that is important to our generation. That type of diverse collaboration will be recognized and long remembered leading to a loyal generation of consumers for many years to come."

34. Lipinski, P. (2018, January 3). 3 Ways Gen Z Will Start to Change the Workplace in 2018. Retrieved from https://www.hrtech-nologist.com/articles/performance-management/3-ways-gen-z-will-start-to-change-the-workplace-in-2018/

LESSON 33

COMPENSATE YOUR INTERNS

" As students, we constantly hear about the importance of gaining real-world experience and we are eager to gain that experience," said Ryan Stiesi, a member of the Rutgers University class of 2019. "However, companies and organizations need to understand that we will deliver value as interns and in return for that value, Gen Zers are looking to be compensated with meaningful responsibilities, experiences, mentorship and pay, yes pay." Take notice corporate America, for those companies and organizations who equate Gen Z with free labor and menial tasks, you are going to lose the opportunity to collaborate with an innovative generation who can deliver tremendous value and drive positive business impact.

LESSON 34

WE VALUE PEER-TO-PEER MENTORSHIP

"Whether you call it peer-to-peer advising or peer-to-peer mentorship, we are highly motivated when we are paired with other Gen Zers on projects, programs and assignments because we don't want to let each other down," said Carmen Sclafani, a member of the Rutgers University class of 2019. "In starting a peer-to-peer education and athletic development initiative on campus, we were able to measure success when Gen Zers collaborated together on internship and career programs compared to when they were advised by older generations." Any company, big or small, should listen to Carmen and launch a Gen Z peer-to-peer mentorship program in a way that it can be measured for success.

LESSON 35

EFFICIENCY IS EXTRA IMPORTANT TO US

❝We are not going to take time out of our day to go to an actual store to shop when we can make the same purchase using our mobile phone while we are commuting to our internship or in between classes," said Ashley Rose, a member of the University of Mississippi class of 2020. "Other generations may consider us lazy, but we value our time tremendously and we look to accomplish all tasks in the most efficient way to get them done without wasting time." In an article in Forbes, Kyle Elliott commented on Gen Zers focus on efficiency, saying, "Those who belong to Generation Z, even more so than the millennial generation, appreciate the great value that technology and subsequently efficiency, bring to the workplace. Those companies that focus their efforts on technology and improving efficiency will...recruit top talent and beat out their competition."[35]

35. Council, F. C. (2018, February 27). Here Comes Gen Z: How To Attract And Retain The Workforce's Newest Generation. Retrieved from https://www.forbes.com/sites/forbescoachescouncil/2018/02/27/here-comes-gen-z-how-to-attract-and-retain-the-workforces-newest-generation/#75eed27c1b2e

PART IV

SLIDING INTO GEN Z'S MEDIA PREFERENCES

LESSON 36

YOU WON'T REACH US THROUGH TRADITIONAL MEDIA

" Gen Z, the newest generation of teens graduating into adulthood, isn't just snubbing print, but have abandoned old media altogether, choosing to get their news from Instagram, YouTube and Facebook, according to a global study of those 18-32."[36] The shift in the types of media Gen Z consumes is overwhelmingly in the favor of digital media, and traditional media is nearly extinct with this generation according to a survey of Gen Zers by Hawk Communications, the student-run public relations agency at Montclair State University. More than 40% of Gen Zers never read a newspaper, more than 50% read a magazine only a few times of year, more than 30% only watch network and cable television a few times a week with more than 15% never watching it or only watching it a few times a year. Instead, more than 75% of Gen Zers are turning to Twitter, news apps like The Skimm, web sites and Snapchat for news and information and more than 75% prefer Netflix and YouTube for viewing video content over network and cable television.[37] "We don't have time to sit through commercials or scroll through lengthy stories," said Carly Galasso, a 2018 graduate of Rutgers University. "We like to consume content that is immediate and concise, and traditional media isn't built that way."

---

36. Bedard, P. (2018, February 20). Gen Z abandons old media, choose Instagram, YouTube, Facebook. Retrieved from https://www. washingtonexaminer.com/gen-z-abandons-old-media-choose-instagram-youtube-facebook

37. Hawk Communications, Montclair State University, Generation Z Survey conducted online via Google, April-June, 2018

LESSON 37

TELEVISION PROGRAMMING IS ANTIQUATED

"Watching live cable news is virtually non-existent amongst Gen Zers. Watching an hour-long news show seems antiquated when we get our headlines throughout the day instantaneously on our phones," said David Casadonte, a 2018 graduate of Fordham University. "As for watching network television, Gen Zers undoubtedly prefer watching their content on streaming platforms like Netflix, Hulu and Amazon." A survey of Gen Zers by Montclair State University's student-run public relations agency, Hawk Communications, validated this sentiment. According to the survey, 10% of Gen Zers only watch network or cable television a few times a year while 14% watch it once a month and 22% watch once a week while 5% claim they never watch mainstream television options. When it comes to their preferred source of viewing content according to the same survey, only 10% selected network or cable television, yet 75% of Gen Zers prefer viewing original content on Netflix and YouTube.[38]

38. Hawk Communications, Montclair State University, Generation Z Survey conducted online via Google, April-June, 2018

LESSON 38

WE LISTEN...JUST DIFFERENTLY

Whether large head phones or wireless ear buds, Gen Z listens to audio content, it's just a different listening experience than previous generations. According to a Gen Z study by Hawk Communications, the student-run public relations agency at Montclair State University, more than 40% listen to AM/FM radio only once a week or less with 8% never listening to the stations on the radio dial. Instead, an overwhelming 80% are listening to music streaming services like Spotify or Apple Music.[39] A survey of 500 female Gen Zers by Sweety High called out Spotify (61%) as the most popular source for listening to music.[40] In fact, when it comes to their mobile phone, more than 70% said they primarily use their phone to listen to music and podcasts according to the Hawk Communications survey. "We prefer music and podcast streaming because it allows us to take control of what we are listening to and customizing it based on our mood, time of day or even location," said Ashley Rose, a member of the class of 2020 at the University of Mississippi.

39. Hawk Communications, Montclair State University, Generation Z Survey conducted online via Google, April-June, 2018

40. Hodak, B. (2018, March 07). New Study Spotlights Gen Z's Unique Music Consumption Habits. Retrieved from https://www.forbes.com/sites/brittanyhodak/2018/03/06/new-study-spotlights-gen-zs-unique-music-consumption-habits/#778b58f842d0

LESSON 39

I WANT MY NEWS &
I WANT IT NOW

In a 2018 survey of Generation Z by Montclair State University's student-run public relations agency, Hawk Communications, more than 50% of Gen Zers said their primary source of news and information is either Twitter (31.9%) or news apps (23.2%).[41] "We want to be able to review headlines quickly on our phones and then determine if we want to access the full story, so Twitter delivers that in a format that works well for Gen Z and news app like The Skimm were built for Gen Z," commented Summer Beal, a 2018 graduate of East Stroudsburg University. In that same Hawk Communications survey, 37% of Gen Zers said they never read a newspaper, more than 20% never read a magazine and more than 40% are only watching network or cable television once a week or once a month. Media companies that are going to thrive with Gen Z are those that deliver news where Gen Z is consuming media - Twitter, Snapchat, Instagram and news apps - in easy-to-digest summaries, lists and 10-second reads.

41. Hawk Communications, Montclair State University, Generation Z Survey conducted online via Google, April-June, 2018

LESSON 40

THE HEADLINE MUST GRAB OUR ATTENTION

Whether CNN Breaking New, FOX Now, ESPN or any other news source, Gen Z does consume news. They just receive it and consume it differently than previous generations. "I get my news via information and sports apps. When the news arrives on my phone, I decide if I want to learn more or search for additional information based mostly on the headline. If I do opt-in for more information, I then decide if I believe it is valuable enough to share with my followers on social media," said Jake Panus, a member of the class of 2022 at Fairfield Ludlowe High School. Christina Hamdan, a member of the University of Delaware class of 2019, added, "The headline is very important especially if it jumps out and captures my attention. I prefer CNN Breaking News updates and Twitter for my news and information and from those sources, I will pick and choose what content I want to read, view or listen to."

LESSON 41

YOU HAVE SECONDS TO GET OUR ATTENTION

" Although their options are practically endless, their time is not – they (Gen Z) have an average attention span of eight seconds as compared to 12 seconds for millennials."[42]

With the introduction of six-second commercials by FOX and other television networks as well as social media platforms including Snapchat, it should come as no surprise that it has been well documented that the attention span of Gen Zers is eight seconds or less. "Businesses attempting to tap into Generation Z will have to do so with exceptionally pithy advertising. This is a generation accustomed to emjois, hashtags…so if businesses can not communicate the big picture in just a few words, they will have lost the attention of their desired audience."[43] For marketers, that means you need to do something disruptive and attention-grabbing in the first few seconds of video content or in the headline of a story. "If you don't grab my attention in the first five seconds, I am not going to invest my time to consume a brand's content," said Summer Beal, a 2018 graduate of East Stroudsburg University. "Branded content doesn't need to be sensational. However, it needs to be highly relevant for the Gen Z audience as well as still being authentic to what the brand stands for."

---

42. Grigoreva, G. (2017, November 27). How To Win The Hearts Of The Gen Z Consumer Base In Eight Seconds. Retrieved from https://www.forbes.com/sites/forbescommunicationscouncil/2017/11/27/how-to-win-the-hearts-of-the-gen-z-consumer-base-in-eight-seconds/#7f89330e6bff

43. Capatides, C. (2015, September 22). Meet Generation Z. Retrieved from https://www.cbsnews.com/pictures/meet-generation-z/16/

LESSON 42

OUR TIME IS VALUABLE

While the oldest Gen Zers are just entering the workforce, the majority are still in college, high school and middle school where they are juggling school, part-time jobs, extracurricular activities, volunteering, internships and socializing. There is very little time to consume media and content, but Gen Zers want to consume content on their time and schedule. In a Trifecta Research survey, 59% of Gen Z video consumption content is done via over-the-top (OOT) services as opposed to 29% for television.[44] "Our 24/7 schedules do not allow us to watch or participate in scheduled programming. It's why we all watch Netflix, because it allows us to maximize what little free time we have," said Jessica Ortega, a member of the Montclair State University class of 2018. "National morning shows, and the evening news don't exist in our world and we are getting the majority of our late-night content through video shorts of Kimmel, Corden and Fallon the next day through our social media channels when we have a few minutes between our priorities to check-in."

---

44. Generation Z Media Consumption Habits (n.d.). Trifecta Research. Retrieved from http://trifectaresearch.com/wp-content/uploads/2015/09Generation-Z-Sample-Trifecta-Reserach-Deliverable.pdf

LESSON 43

LONG FORM CONTENT STILL HAS SOME APPEAL

While Gen Zers prefer text over email and efficient communication over long-winded conversations, long form content does have a place with this generation. "While the news has been condensed to tweets and 15-second videos, I believe Gen Zers are bucking the trend and have a craving for long form content. Just look at podcast interviews and even Game of Thrones," said Christian Glew, a 2018 graduate if the University of Alabama. "I think we are craving that extra level of understanding we gain from spending more time with content to learn more."

LESSON 44

NOT ALL SOCIAL MEDIA IS THE SAME

When it comes to Gen Z, as a marketer or media, never make the mistake of believing that all social medial platforms serve the same purpose. In a study conducted by Atlanta-based Response Media, a digital-customer relationship management agency, it is detailed what each popular social media platform delivers to Gen Z. According to the study, Instagram provides a channel to showcase their aspirational self while Snapchat delivers real-time, unfiltered life moments. Twitter delivers news and a newsfeed in a timely manner and Facebook, while not as popular with Gen Z, still offers information when needed.[45] As a marketer or media company, when it comes to Gen Z, no one piece of original content can simply be replicated across various social media channels. Content needs to be customized for specific social media platforms based on how Gen Z engages with content while on a specific channel. "For us Gen Zers, not all social media channels function the same," said Carly Galasso, a 2018 graduate of Rutgers University. "I love Snapchat because of the real-time factor, while I use Instagram to share my favorite moment of the day and Twitter gives me news and headlines."

---

45. Generation Z - The Newest Generation. (n.d.). Retrieved June 17, 2016, from http://www.responsemedia.com/gen-z/

LESSON 45

YOU CAN FIND US ON MORE THAN FIVE SCREENS

❝ Gen Z consumes and processes content much faster than other generations, in particular, because of apps like Snapchat with its 10-second story limit. Gen Zers are very good at quickly sorting through vast amounts of information using five screens simultaneously: smartphones, tablets, TVs, laptops and desktops.”[46] If you are looking to find and engage Gen Z with a marketing message, it won't be easy. It has been well documented that Gen Z bounces between at least five screens - smartphone, tablet, laptop, desktop, watch, video game console and television – that is actually seven screens. “Generation Z doesn't just have a shorter attention span; they also juggle more screens. On average, millennials bounce between 3 screens at a time - which is why television commercials are seen as poor marketing strategies for reaching these attention-scattered viewers. However, things aren't getting less complicated: Generation Z tends to juggle 5 screens at once!”[47] Not only does Gen Z feel very comfortable transitioning from one screen to another depending on the need, time and location, they do it on their time and schedule so strategically planning to intercept Gen Z as they move from one screen to the next is not something that can easily be planned. “Being able to hand-pick the content I exclusively want to consume, along with being able to watch it regardless of my location and even live and on-the-go

46. Grigoreva, G. (2017, November 27). How To Win The Hearts Of The Gen Z Consumer Base In Eight Seconds. Retrieved from https://www.forbes.com/sites/forbescommunicationscouncil/2017/11/27/how-to-win-the-hearts-of-the-gen-z-consumer-base-in-eight-seconds/#7aac9df36bff

47. Patel, D. (2017, November 27). 5 D ifferences Between Marketing To M illennials V s . Gen Z. Retrieved from https://www.forbes.com/sites/deeppatel/2017/11/27/5-d ifferences- between- marketing- to -m illennials-v s - gen-z/

is really changing the media consumption game for Gen Z," commented Ryan Rose, a 2017 graduate of Rutgers University. "Although I don't have a cable package, I feel more connected to my interests than ever before, through leveraging the multi-screen capabilities available to Gen Z and all consumers."

LESSON 46

YOUTUBE IS THE EPICENTER OF OUR GENERATION

Aside from learning via endless YouTube videos that tutor Gen Zers about any topic they can imagine, YouTube offers so much more including haul videos and unboxing content. "YouTube is the epicenter of my generation. It is so much more than just videos that teach us," commented Sophia Kazee, a member of the University of Pittsburgh class of 2021. "YouTubers who are Gen Zers are now celebrities and we want to be like them. I am on YouTube all day, viewing the beauty and fashion videos. I love the haul videos which features items a YouTuber purchased, and they provide the details including pricing. YouTube caters to all of our interests from fashion and cooking to budgeting and studying and YouTube partners with many brands in a way that is engaging, especially when they offer special pricing codes." Brand marketers would be wise to develop and integrate a YouTube element in their Gen Z content marketing strategy if they have not already considered that approach.

LESSON 47

YOUTUBE IS OUR TUTOR

According to a Gen Z survey conducted by Hawk Communications, the student-run public relations agency at Montclair State University, YouTube is second only to Netflix as the preferred source for watching video content. More than 32% of Gen Zers prefer YouTube for their video content over network and cable television and popular streaming channels.[48] According to Trifecta Research, Gen Z watches more than two hours of YouTube each day.[49] "We go to YouTube for tutorials on just about every possible topic from food to fashion and technology to travel," commented Katelyn Woebse, a member of the Montclair State University class of 2020. "There is a tutorial for everything and we want to learn everything. We are a generation of explorers." Marketers and brands who are challenged with engaging Gen Zers because of their propensity for viewing content via channels like Netflix and YouTube would be well served producing a meaningful Gen Z tutorial content strategy on YouTube.

48. Hawk Communications, Montclair State University, Generation Z Survey conducted online via Google, April-June, 2018

49. Granados, N. (2017, June 22). Gen Z Media Consumption: It's A Lifestyle, Not Just Entertainment. Retrieved from https://www.forbes.com/sites/nelsongranados/2017/06/20/gen-z-media-consumption-its-a-lifestyle-not-just-entertainment/#71b8ca9118c9

LESSON 48

WE USE SOCIAL MEDIA TO EDUCATE & INFORM

" I love to do my make-up and have a passion for putting every single detail on Instagram where I can share with Gen Zers around the world, and they can respond and react," said Elissa Edwards, a member of the SUNY Old Westbury class of 2020. "I try to produce and distribute weekly content to help and inform others. Ultimately, I hope to share informative content daily. I go into great details about the products I use, how I use them and none of these brands are compensating me, but I am serving as an online advocate for their products." Marketers would be wise if they partnered with Gen Zers who are micro influencers like Elissa, giving her an even larger platform to fuel her passion to produce and share content that appeals to Gen Zers around the world.

LESSON 49

SOCIAL MEDIA OPENS THE WORLD TO US

"I have met many people around the world through social media that other generations have just never experienced. The world is actually a much smaller place. We learn so much about other cultures through social media," said Sophie Kleinberg, a member of The Beacon School class of 2021. "When I meet someone at an event or another location, I turn to social media to discover as much as I can about their passions. By scrolling through their Instagram content or reviewing their tweets, I can learn more than ever before about someone. Previous generations never had that type of access to get to know someone to the extent that we do, and it drives a global community of connections for us."

LESSON 50

SOCIAL MEDIA & CONTENT SPURS HEALTH & WELLNESS

"Health and wellness is a priority for Gen Z as social media and the sharing of photos and videos makes us much more conscious of our bodies and appearance. We face pressure to fulfill a healthy image and social media provides easy access to training, workouts and fitness content that we can quickly view and use," said Kaitlyn Matthews, a member of the Rutgers University class of 2019. Her classmate, Courtney Copeland added, "With recent documentaries such as 'What the Health' and 'Forks Over Knives,' our generation is much more aware of what we are putting in our bodies and we are influencing the shift to organic foods and reading labels. Brands like Whole Foods and Traders Joe's know this, and they are marketing to Gen Zers to shop organic and eat healthy." Brooke Stern, a member of the Cornell University class of 2019, added, "Gen Zers like to work out and eat well. It makes us think better and feel better. It's why exercise technology like Nike Plus, the Apple watch and fitbit are so popular with our generation. Exercise is an essential part of my day as I always make it a priority during the week to get in my exercise and often share my workout experiences with other Gen Zers through my social media channels in a way that inspires others to do the same."

PART V

THE WAVE FOR BRAND MARKETERS

LESSON 51

WE ENGAGE WITH BRANDS

Nearly 30% of GenZers actively seek out brands based on values, reports a study titled, "Dollars and Change: Young People Tap Brands as Agents of Social Change," from the non-profit consultancy, DoSomething Strategic.[50] Unlike previous generations, Gen Zers I interviewed told me they are taking an active interest in how brands are marketing themselves to this generation from social media content to the causes they support. "We expect brands to market to us, but if they truly want to engage us, they need to do it in an authentic Gen Z kind of way and inject their brand into our lives across work, friends, passions, causes and social media," said 2017 Rutgers University graduate Melissa Jannuzzi. "When I get together with my friends, we talk about what brands are doing to market to us and the promotions they are offering." No brand is applauded more for the content they serve up to Gen Z than Wendy's. Mashable captured Wendy's authentic approach to their popular Twitter handle writing, "the team creates personalized, thought-provoking witty responses that sound like they came from your sassy best friend."[51] Another Gen Zer commented to me, "Wendy's content is relatable, entertaining and funny and that's one sure way to engage Gen Z."

50. Brands Take Note: Gen Z Is Putting Its Money Where Its Values Are. (2018, May 8). Retrieved from http://www.sustainable-brands.com/news_and_views/walking_talk/sustainable_brands/brands_take_note_gen_z_putting_its_money_where_its

51. Gallucci, N. (2017, January 05). Behold: The sass master behind Wendy's Twitter. Retrieved from https://mashable.com/2017/01/05/sassy-wendys-social-media-manager/#vX.7THlMkiqz

LESSON 52

LOCATION, LOCATION, LOCATION IS IMPORTANT

It should come as no surprise that for many Gen Zers, Snapchat is among their most popular social media platforms, but it's location-based features like Snap Map or Find My Friends from Apple that truly engages Gen Z. "The truth is that teens *care* about where their friends are and what they are doing, as it provides very important **context** to how they may and 'should' interact with their friends."[52] There is no longer a need to plan to meet someone in advance. Instead, location-based apps allow Gen Z to meet-up spontaneously anywhere especially at major events, destinations or parties. "No matter the location, I can discover if my friends are at the same event or nearby which leads to a spontaneous and immediate meet-up without the hassle of planning," said Alexa Restaino, a communications major in the Rutgers University class of 2019. "Our generation enjoys discovery through spontaneous get-togethers, and apps like Find My Friends allows for that no matter the time or distance it takes to have an unplanned meet-up," said Ashley Rose, a member of the class of 2020 at the University of Mississippi. Brand marketers who can harness the power and appeal of location-based technology can create meaningful pop-up activations on-location spontaneously that result in real-time Gen Z interaction and engagement.

---

52. Stuto, G. (2017, August 08). Here's how Gen-Z actually uses Snap Map and why it
    could be big for discovery. Retrieved from https://medium.com/@giuseppestuto/
    heres-how-gen-z-actually-uses-snap-map-and-why-it-could-be-big-for-discovery-b39c5bd46155

LESSON 53

WE ARE EDUCATED CONSUMERS

"An educated consumer is our best customer," may be an old advertising tag line for a clothing retailer, but it is back in fashion with Gen Z. "One comment about Gen Z being frugal: They aren't frugal. They spend their money reasonably. They are practical when it comes to so many things that we were spend-thrifts on. But they spend their money carefully and openly on what they want, and they are willing to do it."[53] Stephanie Michael, a member of the Montclair State University class of 2019 commented, "We are on such limited budgets, that we are not just giving our money away. Brands and companies should be on notice that we will conduct extensive, in-depth research before we make a purchase. I will only invest my money in quality products that have received positive reviews from media, family and other Gen Zers."

53. Blair, A. (2018, March 12). How Will Gen Z Reshape Retail? - Retail TouchPoints. Retrieved from https://www.retailtouch-points.com/features/trend-watch/how-will-gen-z-reshape-retail

LESSON 54

JOIN OUR MOVEMENT

"One of the most effective ways a brand can engage with Gen Z is to truly join our movements around social, community and political causes," said Sabrina Araullo, a 2018 graduate of Montclair State University. "Brands can't simply pander to us. They need to demonstrate that they authentically think like us and believe in causes that are important in our Gen Z world, society and culture, today, tomorrow and for many years ahead. They need to demonstrate a commitment to these causes and in return, they will earn loyal advocates and customers." A study of Gen Z girls conducted by Girl Up, in collaboration with Marie Claire, reinforces Sabrina's point-of-view with 65% expecting brands to take a stand on social issues and the same amount believe buying from brands that give back to the community is important.[54]

---

54. DiTrolio, M. (2018, June 07). Gen Z May Be the Socially Conscious Generation of Girls Yet. Retrieved from https://www.marieclaire.com/culture/a21099780/girl-up-study-gen-z/

LESSON 55

GIVE US AN EXPERIENCE TO SHARE

❝ Gen Z craves authentic brand experiences, something tangible and tactile. They also are generally categorized as favoring memories and experiences as opposed to owning material goods."[55]. Listen up brands and brand marketers, Gen Z is eager to engage with your brand via unique experiences. "If you look at the content we share on our social media channels, it is primarily experienced-based," said, Jessica Ortega, a member of the Montclair State University class of 2019. "Brands should start focusing more on experiential marketing. It's not only less in-your-face advertising, but Gen Z will share the branded content and advocate on a brand's behalf without the direct payment that online influencers increasingly require." Gen Z has moved past storytelling and is interested in experiencing brands through "story living." Mike Morra, a 2017 graduate of Manhattan College, added, "It feels like music festivals, theater groups and other major cultural dictators are pushing us towards creating distorted or alternative realities in physical spaces and Gen Z is driving this. Gen Z wants to be active participants in events and experiences."

---

55. Generation Z craves experiential marketing. Here's Why. (2017, October 27). Retrieved from http://www.inphantry.com/generation-z-craves-experiential-marketing-heres-why/

LESSON 56

WE WANT TO BE FIRST

❝ It is a badge of honor for Gen Zers to be the first in their social network to share content, news and information and that includes everything from branded content that might be clever or funny to a great promotional offer for a product or service," said Summer Beal, a 2018 graduate of East Stroudsburg University. "While we may not have the massive reach of celebrities and social media superstars, brands looking to engage Gen Z should seriously consider a grassroots effort with actual members of Gen Z, micro influencers, who have influence and credibility in our social circles with thousands of very close friends. Those brands that give us the news first, will drive great engagement with those who trust us most, our Gen Z friends who follow our social media channels."

LESSON 57

UNDERSTAND OUR FINANCES

The oldest Gen Zers have just entered the workforce and are stretching their first paychecks to pay off their college loans and most likely their first rent and utility bills since graduating. The remainder of Generation Z is working part-time jobs to pay for college tuition and room and board or saving up for that first car and gas money. According to an Ernst & Young survey of Gen Zers, when it comes to brands and retailers, what is most important is free shipping and delivery (80%), and special rates or discounts (77%).[56] "We are broke," said Katelyn Woebse, a member of the Montclair State University class of 2020. "We are looking to engage with brands that understand our financial situation and come to us with special offers and promotions. Brands that go beyond what is expected and do that something extra for Gen Z could have loyal customers for a lifetime." That point-of-view is supported by a survey of Gen Zers conducted by Hawk Communications, the student-run public relations agency at Montclair State University, in which more than 60% confirmed that they were influenced to make a purchase or take some sort of action because of a brand's special offer or promotion featured on their respective owned media channels.[57] "Our generation is trying to maximize every dollar we have so we look to brands like Marshalls and TJ Maxx that offer value and affordable products for many of us who are students or recent graduates paying tuition, room and board and student loans," added Amanda Peacock, a member of the class of 2021 at Montclair State University.

56. Tirico, K. (n.d.). Gen Z Is Frugal And Demands Personalization - Retail TouchPoints. Retrieved May 03, 2016, from https://www.retailtouchpoints.com/features/trend-watch/gen-z-is-frugal-and-demands-personalization

57. Hawk Communications, Montclair State University, Generation Z Survey conducted online via Google, April-June, 2018

LESSON 58

WE WANT BRANDS TO ENTERTAIN US

Nearly 40% of Gen Zers follow the social media channels of brands primarily for clever, informative and engaging content reported a Gen Z survey conducted by Hawk Communications, the student-run public relations agency at Montclair State University.[58] "Brands should seek to develop clever and cool concepts with Gen Z relevance. If executed properly my generation will not only be engaged in the moment, but we will eagerly share the experiences with our friends and followers" said Micah Lebowitz, a 2018 graduate of Rutgers University. "Pizza Hut's Pie Tops, Arizona Beverages apparel line, M&M's Bite-Sized Beats and Google Doodles all prove that when marketed effectively, Gen Zers will engage. To ensure our response, it has to be done in an attention-grabbing way, well-crafted for our generation. My recommendation to every brand marketer who is looking to engage and win over Gen Zers for the next decade is to recruit their own diverse Gen Z panel. The panel's thoughts and feedback will help ensure organizations' inspired marketing innovations are not only on brand, but in fact, on target." If you are listening marketers, there is no more valuable advice and counsel than what Micah just offered pro bono.

---

58. Hawk Communications, Montclair State University, Generation Z Survey conducted online via Google, April-June, 2018

LESSON 59

HORSE RACING IS HAPPENING

Of all the lessons I learned from Gen Zers, this one surprised me the most as I heard it from a large enough sample that I thought it was worth sharing. While the sport of horse racing enjoyed its greatest popularity many years ago, it is enjoying a resurgence with Gen Z and many of them aren't even watching the horses race. "Horse racing is one of those unique experiences where you can gather a large group of friends, and get dressed up and socialize in a highly Instagramable setting," said Alexa Restaino, a member of the Rutgers University class of 2019. So, whether it's horse racing, a food truck festival or a multi-day concert, Gen Zers are seeking unique experiences to socialize with friends in venues that offer a compelling backdrop for photo and video capturing and sharing. Brand marketers should look to engage Gen Z at these high traffic intersections of socializing and sharing.

LESSON 60

MINIMALISM MEANS MORE

Less is more when it comes to Gen Z and what they would like to see from brands and marketers as it relates to visual branding and identity. "Gen Z loves photographing and sharing branding, packages and products that are simply designed and branded as it requires no editing," said Stephanie Michael, a member of the class of 2019 at Montclair State University. "If a logo or packaging is too complicated and requires too much work to edit and share, the brand is missing out on a sharable opportunity. Rook Coffee and by Chloe are two brands that are designed for Gen Zers to share on their social media channels and marketers should take notice." Gen Zers repeatedly have confirmed they want to engage with brands and advocate on their behalf, but logos, packages and designs that are overly branded are not going to find their way into Gen Zers sharable content.

LESSON 61

PEOPLE, PLACES, EXPERIENCES & MEMORIES ARE OUR PRIORITY

"We prioritize people, places, experiences and memories over materials goods," said Ashley Rose, a member of the University of Mississippi class of 2020. "We tend to spend our money on experiences rather than products, ultimately trying to strike a balance between now and the future when it comes to our finances. While we may not be as focused as previous generations on saving every dollar for retirement, we try to balance the dollars we do have on memorable experiences we can enjoy today with friends while saving for experiences in the future." Inphantry, a design and branding agency, writes, "Gen Z craves authentic brand experiences, something tangible and tactile. They also are generally categorized as favoring memories and experiences as opposed to owning material goods which is making experiential marketing supremely important to these consumers."[59]

---

59. Generation Z craves experiential marketing. Here's Why. (2017, October 27). Retrieved from http://www.inphantry.com/generation-z-craves-experiential-marketing-heres-why/

LESSON 62

STOP EMAILING US

" Don't email me," said Zoe Butchen, a member of the University of Connecticut class of 2022. "Unless it is interactive and interesting, we are just deleting your emails especially when they arrive daily. After I purchase products from a few brands, I receive daily emails. That is such counter-productive marketing. Instead, get more innovative in your marketing approach and give me special access to something." Rahima Tokhi, a member of the Rutgers University class of 2018 added, "There's nothing more annoying than going into my email first thing when I wake up and I have to delete at least 20 marketing emails from brands and companies. It's especially annoying when it's the same company sending me the same email multiple times in the same day. I will unsubscribe and will not regret my decision. Email Gen Z only if you actually have something useful and unique to offer that meets a Gen Z need or want."

LESSON 63

POP-UPS PRESENT PHOTO OPPS

Brands that create pop-up experiences like Refinery 29's "29 Rooms" which offers 29 installations in one interactive house of style, culture, and technology, engage Gen Z and lend themselves well to social media content that is highly sharable among Gen Zers. "Pop-up events fulfill our social media need and appetite to capture and share content from unique settings and experiences," said Brooke Stern, a member of the Cornell University class of 2019. "Brand marketers should prioritize events and experiences, especially pop-up interactions, if they are looking to engage Gen Zers." Shelby Fong, a member of the Rutgers University class of 2019, added, "brands that are going to be most successful with Gen Z are those that activate through pop-up shows and events like the Museum of Ice Cream and the Pint Shop that allow Gen Zers to be engaged and immersed in interactive experiences that they can capture and share on their social media channels."

LESSON 64

FOOD MAKES FOR GREAT FODDER

For Gen Z, whether it is the actual food, the restaurant or just the culinary environment, they love to produce and share content around food and food experiences. "Food festivals and food experiences like the popular Smorgasburg in Brooklyn, New York offer Gen Zers an endless amount of compelling and engaging content possibilities," said Brooke Stern, a member of the Cornell University class of 2019. Sally Meli, a 2017 graduate of Wagner College added, "Acai bowls were not a thing on the east coast until a couple of years ago. Once people started to Instagram and Snapchat their colorful Acai bowl images, everyone wanted to be part of the trend. Fast forward a few years, and it seems that there is an Acai shop everywhere. Discovering food based on social media content is much more common than finding it anywhere else for Gen Z. I may not even try a restaurant if they do not have appealing food content on social media. It's gotten to the point where many popular restaurants even have 'Instafamous' food accounts that have thousands of followers."

LESSON 65

WE MOVE FAST

" If you are a brand marketer, you need to get ahead of Gen Z. In other words, you need to interview us and listen closely and understand what trends we are forecasting six to 12 months into the future. We move faster than any generation before us and if you are planning some sort of marketing campaign today to engage Gen Z, there is a good chance it will be old news by the time you go to market with it unless you get ahead of the Gen Z curve," said Derek Drotman, a member of the Penn State class of 2020.

LESSON 66

GIVE US PEER-TO-PEER ENTREPRENEURIAL PLATFORMS

If marketers want to satisfy Gen's Z entrepreneurial spirit and their desire to conduct peer-to-peer business, they should look no further than DePop, a peer-to-peer social shopping app based in London that is gaining traction with teens worldwide. "DePop is very cool and allows Gen Zers to start their own business and create their own unique niche in selling products," said Sophie Kleinberg, a member of The Beacon School class of 2021. Eighty percent of DePop's users are under 25.[60] DePop's CEO Maria Raga explained to Forbes why the platform is so appealing to Gen Z. "They want to feel unique, to shop with (and from) friends and to build their own green business without losing a drop of street cred." Kleinberg, a high school sophomore, added, "It's Instagram-like and allows us to build our own business as we are a generation of entrepreneurs."

60. Knowles, K. (2018, April 26). Depop CEO: Solving 3 Big Problems For Young Cool Shoppers. Retrieved from https://www.forbes.com/sites/kittyknowles/2018/04/26/depop-ceo-solving-3-big-problems-for-young-cool-shoppers/#96a31297b40c

LESSON 67

DIFFERENT PLATFORMS CALL FOR DIFFERENT MESSAGING & CONTENT

While Gen Zers have been very vocal that each social media platform plays a different role in their content and media consumption routines, they are also savvy enough to tell marketers they need to strategically message them based on their usage. "I use Spotify when I'm driving and when I am running and working out, so brands who are looking to engage me and other Gen Zers on that specific channel should be looking to customize and create marketing messages that are going to be highly relevant when I am active on Spotify," said Ryan Stiesi, a member of the Rutgers University class of 2019. "It's critical for marketers to get away from a mass message approach and instead, develop channel-specific messages and content that doesn't disrupt our use of a specific channel or platform like Snapchat, Instagram Twitter or YouTube. Their marketing and content should flow seamlessly on each channel so that it naturally fits with the other content we are consuming."

LESSON 68

EDUCATIONAL CONTENT CAN BE MORE USEFUL THAN POPULAR CONTENT

Generation Z enjoys a good laugh as much as the next generation, but that doesn't mean that a funny video short delivers any real value. "We are a generation of learners. We are young and have an endless appetite to learn as much as possible," said Ryan Stiesi, a member of the Rutgers University class of 2019. "Brands and marketers should begin to think about producing content that is informative and educational, and of course, Gen Z relevant. No brand that I am aware of is doing that right now and Gen Zers will see value in it if the content is produced using a Gen Z mindset." Marketers take notice - by collaborating with Gen Zers to produce content that informs and educates Gen Zers, you are taking advantage of an opportunity to engage Gen Z in a way that they currently aren't witnessing and experiencing.

LESSON 69

DON'T FOOL US WITH ECO-CHIC MARKETING

In a column in Forbes, Deep Patel writes, "A characteristic shared by many Gen Zers is the desire to make a positive impact on the world. To that end, Gen Zers are passionate about environmental causes."[61] Gabrielle Liguori, a member of the class of 2019 at Rutgers University, agrees, but offers caution. "Gen Z is definitely environmentally-minded and aware of the real threat of climate change, but we also can fall victim to eco-chic marketing and buy into brands that market and sell eco-friendly campaigns and products. However, if our generation really wants to have a positive impact on the environment, we need to collectively cut back on consumption and waste in general and set an example for all generations."

61. Patel, D. (2017, October 05). 11 Environmental Causes Gen Z Is Passionate About. Retrieved from https://www.forbes.com/sites/deeppatel/2017/10/04/11-environmental-causes-gen-z-is-passionate-about/#22e884b91849

PART VI

THE DOPE ON TECH, APPS & SOCIAL MEDIA

LESSON 70

TEXT ME IF YOU NEED ME

❝ The constant use of our phones allows us to communicate by text very quickly as we have come to expect an immediate response. In our minds, we feel this gives us greater efficiency," commented Brendan Deal, Monroe Township High School class of 2019. When trying to communicate with Gen Z, texting is your best option. Inc. cited a study in which nearly 75% of Gen Zers and millennials in the United States prefer communicating via text.[62] In a Gen Z survey conducted by Hawk Communications, the student-run public relations agency at Montclair State University, nearly 70% of Gen Zers overwhelmingly prefer communicating by text over a phone call (17%) and FaceTime (10%). In that same survey, 99% of Gen Zers claim that texting is how they primarily use their mobile phone. In a comparison between texting and a messenger app, the results weren't even close with 91% preferring to text.[63] "We see texting as not only more efficient since we are constantly on the move, but it's also a great alternative to a phone call if you are an introvert or you find yourself in a crowded public space where it is difficult to hear," said Ashley Rose, a member of the class of 2020 at the University of Mississippi.

62. Jr, B. M. (2017, October 26). Millennials and Gen Z Would Rather Text Each Other Than Do This, According to a New Study. Retrieved from https://www.inc.com/bill-murphy-jr/millennials-gen-z-prefer-texting-to-human-conversations-new-study-says-plus-5-other-findings.html

63. Hawk Communications, Montclair State University, Generation Z Survey conducted online via Google, April-June, 2018

LESSON 71

FIND US ON OUR PHONES DOING EVERYTHING

According to a 2016 Gen Z survey by Google, the median age Gen Zers got their first smartphone was 12.[64] With that, it may not be surprising that nearly 60% of Gen Zers use their mobile phone for 10 or more hours a day with more than 22% claiming they use it more than 15 hours a day according to a Gen Z survey by Montclair State University's student-run public relations agency Hawk Communications.[65] "For Gen Zers, our phone is our life. I could not imagine being without it for more than an hour. I pay for everything with my phone. I communicate with my phone and I get from one location to another thanks to my phone," said Derek Drotman, a member of the Penn State class of 2020. So, what exactly are Gen Zers doing on their mobile phones for so many hours a day? Just about everything... texting (99%), accessing social media sites (93%), sending emails (70%), listening to music and podcasts (70%), making phone calls (70%), navigating their way to a destination (67%), watching videos (65%) and shooting and sharing videos and photos (64%) are just some of the most popular mobile phone activities for Gen Zers according to the Hawk Communications survey. "A mobile phone is so convenient to have with me at all times. It's portable and fits in my pocket and I can do some unbelievable things from simply texting and FaceTiming to sharing content and shopping," said Pat Kelly, a 2017 graduate of Rutgers University.

---

64. Generation Z: New Insights Into The Mobile First Mindset Of Teens. In Google. Retrieved from https://storage.googleapis.com/think/docs/GenZ_Insights_All_teens.pdf

65. Hawk Communications, Montclair State University, Generation Z Survey conducted online via Google, April-June, 2018

LESSON 72

WE LIVE IN A CASHLESS WORLD

Sixty-nine percent of Gen Zers use a mobile banking app daily or weekly according to the 2017 Accenture Driving The Future of Payments: 10 Mega Trends.[66] Ask Gen Zers if they have cash in their wallet or purse and they will probably ask if you accept Venmo, Zelle or another mobile wallet that lets you easily make payments to friends. "Our generation hardly ever carries cash and we rely on mobile technology like Venmo which makes it very easy to pay someone," said Ashley Rose, a member of the University of Mississippi class of 2020. "I find it especially helpful when I am on campus and come across an opportunity to make a donation or support a cause and I can simply make the payment via my phone." The "Technologies Influencing Generation Z Payment Adoption" report released in 2018 by Javelin Strategy & Research notes, "The convergence of social, shopping, and payments, fed by artificial intelligence, 'plays directly to the habits of the Gen Z consumer.'"[67]

66. 10 Mega Trends Driving Future of Payments | Accenture. (n.d.). Retrieved from https://www.accenture.com/us-en/insight-banking-future-payments-ten-trends

67. Woodward, K. (2018, May 30). Generation Z Emerges With a New Way of Thinking About Payments. Retrieved from https://www.digitaltransactions.net/generation-z-emerges-with-a-new-way-of-thinking-about-payments/

LESSON 73

OUR FAVORITE CURRENCY IS SOCIAL

From products and packaging to events and experiences, Gen Z is eager to engage with brands if they can deliver content that is Gen Z relevant, authentic and balanced – not too commercial, while providing value in the form of social currency. Vivaldi Partners, in a study titled, "Why brands need to build and nurture social currency," wrote about social currency, "it measures the ability of brands to fit into how consumers manage their social lives in today's digital and mobile age."[68] No brand was referenced more by Gen Zers than Wendy's when it comes to brands that understand and deliver best-in-class social currency. "We are not afraid to engage with brands," said Summer Beal, a 2019 graduate of East Stroudsburg. "We proactively look to share content from brands that is relevant to our generation and in our tone and language. That content becomes currency for our own social channels and increases the engagement we have with our friends which is something Gen Zers are always looking for."

68. Social Currency: Why Brands Need To Build And Nurse Social Currency. (2010). Vivaldi Partners. http://images.fastcompany.com/Vivaldi-Partners_Social -Currency.pdf

LESSON 74

OUR PHONES ARE OUR LIFE

" Smart phones are not just for Twitter and Instagram – we are often conducting business on our phone," said Cole Butchen, a member of the Cornell University class of 2019. "Phones are a necessary tool for almost everything we do, ranging from work, school, and managing our social interactions." In a column in Forbes on how Gen Z will change the workforce, Deep Patel wrote, "These young people have always lived in a connected world, and they're used to constant updates from dozens of apps. Switching between different tasks and paying simultaneous attention to a wide range of stimuli comes naturally to them. This can be perfect for a workplace that requires multitasking. If you're looking for employees who can focus deeply on a task for a long period of time, make sure that's communicated to potential Gen Z employees. And, if you see them looking at their phone during work hours, don't assume that will distract them for ages — they're used to spending five seconds checking for updates before returning to the task at hand."[69]

69. Patel, D. (2017, September 22). 8 Ways Generation Z Will Differ From Millennials In The Workplace. Retrieved from https://www.forbes.com/sites/deeppatel/2017/09/21/8-ways-generation-z-will-differ-from-millennials-in-the-workplace/#3ef582ca76e5

LESSON 75

WE WANT SOMEONE TO TALK TO...OR A CHATBOT

❝ Gen Z thrives on efficient communication. For example, when I need information, I would almost always rather have a brief call with an actual person or a highly efficient chatbot rather than be caught in an automated system with countless prompts," said Cole Butchen, a member of the Cornell University class of 2019. "If you need an actionable task, human connection is very important to be able to speak directly to someone and get answers. While it may seem surprising, it speaks to our desire for personalization." Chatbots, "offer the instant gratification that Gen Z demands. They expect real-time communication, not only from their friends and family, but the brands they engage with too."[70]

---

70. The chatbot generation: Marketing your brand to a younger audience. (2018, May 31). Retrieved from http://www.thedrum.com/opinion/2018/05/31/the-chatbot-generation-marketing-your-brand-younger-audience

LESSON 76

WE LOVE GIFS

❝ The use of GIFs and memes makes the simplest text or tweet you attach to it much funnier, which is why they are so popular with Gen Z. It's there for dramatic effect and if done right, you can have it go viral," said Rahima Tokhi, a member of the Rutgers University class of 2018. "I sometimes like to include GIFs even in my powerpoint presentations to keep my classmates engaged because we are a generation known for having short attention spans; especially with our phones near us." Medium captured the popularity of GIFs with Gen Zers in writing, "I'd say that it's the cross between image and video that makes the GIF so incredibly appealing. Regular photos in JPG or PNG format already do fine on social media, because we're quickly moved by visual content, but the GIF format adds something much more special—a mini video, with no sound, that can be watched from start to finish in as little as one or two seconds in a simple, auto-looping fashion."[71]

71. K. (2017, June 12). GIFs and Gen Z – Kweak·ly – Medium. Retrieved from https://medium.com/@kweak/other-post-where-we-share-why-we-are-so-excited-about-gifs-b69d2833a047

LESSON 77

BEING A BITMOJI IS THE BEST

The Bitmoji app, which is owned by Snapchat, was made for Gen Z and their visual Gen Z dialect. "Bitmoji's have been a great addition to the digital space. They add so much fun to conversations, and they are a great way to express creativity. I am in a group chat and we are constantly sending Bitmoji's to one another," said Jenna DeMato, Rutgers University class of 2019. "If I have exciting news to share, I will send it in the group chat and, almost instantly, I will receive a Bitmoji back. More often than not, the Bitmoji replaces words and acts as a response on its own. Incorporating Bitmoji's into our group chats has been so much fun, and it really adds an extra element to the conversation." Ryan Jannuzzi, a 2018 high school graduate added, "Bitmoji's are really trending right now with my friends. We can personalize them and use them to market our personal brands. Brands that bring Bitmoji's to life in the form of apparel and other products and merchandise will realize engagement with Gen Z." A Gen Zer who penned a column for Business Insider, wrote, "Even profile pictures on Snapchat are set to show someone's Bitmoji character by default. The app's consistent stream of fun and integration with one of the biggest Gen Z apps out there continues to make it a hit and keep it high up on the app store."[72]

---

72. C. (2017, August 12). An 18-year-old who just graduated high school explains which apps Gen Z is currently obsessed with. Retrieved from http://www.businessinsider.com/an-18-year-old-explains-which-apps-gen-z-loves-2017-8

LESSON 78

WE EXPRESS OUR EMOTIONS VIA EMOJIS

Face with tears of joy, red heart, loudly crying face, heart eyes face, face throwing a kiss, face with rolling eyes, smiling face with smiling eyes, thinking face – it's an emoji world and Gen Z is living and flourishing in it. "Emojis are half of our communication whether texting or group messaging. It's just an easier way to communicate and it's more fun and lightens up the mood," said Ryan Jannuzzi, Rutgers University class of 2022. "It's just second nature and if brands want to communicate with us, they need to get our emoji language as it is simple, relatable and will get a strong reaction from us." Carly Galasso, Rutgers University class of 2018 added, "Emojis are emotions through text and they are a great way for Gen Zers to express themselves and to show emotion." Joeri Van de Bergh, author of "How Cool Brands Stay Hot," commented about emojis at a youth marketing conference, saying, "They (Gen Z) are the 'emojinal' generation because a picture is worth more than 1,000 words. Brands need to take note of this when they are trying to talk to this generation. Get rid of the boring aspects of marketing because we have a visual generation here."[73]

73. Marketing To Gen Z? No Better Time To Get 'Emojinal'. (2016, September 21). Retrieved from https://www.cmo.com/features/articles/2016/9/21/marketers-targeting-youth-need-to-get-emojinal-yms-conference.html#gs.kxDyfYY

LESSON 79

SEND ME A TELEGRAM FOR A GROUP CHAT

Texting one-on-one is just too easy for Gen Zers so it should come as no surprise that they enjoy juggling simultaneous group conversations. Telegram, a cloud-based instant messaging app, is very popular with teens as is Group Me. "Telegram is the only platform we used in high school. It's a platform built specifically for text messages. I have 15 active chats every day on Telegram. Group chats inspire us as you never know where they may lead," said Ryan Jannuzzi, Rutgers University class of 2022. "My biggest group chat was 50 people." Jenna DeMato, a member of the Rutgers University class of 2019, added, "Group chats, especially through applications like GroupMe, have made communication with others so much easier. I have been in so many group projects in school where we used group chats to communicate. Group chats make everything so much more efficient and convenient. If I want to ask someone a question, all I do is type it and click send. Then, instantly, the entire group is notified. If I need an immediate response, I know that a group chat is the way to go. In my own experience Gen Zers just don't have the time to schedule calls, meet in person, or communicate via email."

LESSON 80

PLEASE RESPECT OUR PRIVACY

While Gen Zers love to socialize and share content with the world, they prioritize privacy. "Gen Z are savvy to the information they're putting out when they're in the digital space. They're switched on to customizing their privacy settings and personal information, and the data shows they'd rather keep that data safe than risk it for peer affirmation or online validation."[74] According to Brian Taylor in a column he wrote on the importance of privacy when it comes to Gen Zers, he cited a survey in which 87% of Gen Zers agreed that keeping their content private was more important than getting "likes." According to Summer Beal, a 2018 graduate of East Stroudsburg University, "Privacy settings vary depending on the social media platform. The majority of Gen Zers set privacy settings on Instagram because we are sharing life moments and only want to share with those who we provide access, while Twitter is a channel where we are typically commenting on news and events and we view that as more of a public platform."

---

74. Jaywing. (2018, March 19). How important is online privacy to Gen Z? Jaywing.com. Retrieved from https://jaywing.com/news/z-5-privacy

LESSON 81

THERE'S AN APP FOR EVERYTHING

"We turn to apps for everything from entertainment and fun to protecting us and getting us to our destination in the most-timely way," said Elissa Edwards, a member of the SUNY Old Westbury class of 2020. "Citizen is a very popular app that monitors 911 police and fire calls. I feel like it protects me as it alerts me about crimes and emergencies in my immediate surroundings. We really don't watch the news and an app like this really can connect us as we are not informed. We are not consuming traditional media so apps like this are very helpful. I also rely on a transit app as it tells me where my trains and busses are. I love this app especially if I am running late. No need for an old fashion schedule. There is no need to ask for directions anymore. We consider our phone and apps powerful tech tools that help us live our lives." Sophia Kazee, a member of the University of Pittsburgh class of 2021, added, "There is an app for everything and everything has a million apps. I even use an app called Forest that has me virtually growing a tree to incentivize me to stay off my phone. The longer I stay off my phone, the more the tree will grow. Forest proves there is an app for virtually anything."

LESSON 82

EDUCATE US ONLINE

Generation Z is leading the change in how learning takes place. They are a driving force in the innovation of new learning tools, teaching styles, and unlimited access to resources. And, they are proving that college is headed in a direction of a more learner-centric environment where students will become the directors of their own futures."[75] Elissa Edwards, a member of the SUNY Old Westbury class of 2020 said," "Online classes and education is the way things are going with our generation. We can manage our time more effectively as the deadlines and deliverables are our responsibilities on our time. I am now finding myself going online to learn lessons beyond the classroom." Brands should consider offering online courses featuring Gen Z passions and interests starring influencers and experts who resonate with Gen Zers.

75. Kozinsky, S. (2017, July 24). How Generation Z Is Shaping The Change In Education. Retrieved from https://www.forbes.com/sites/sievakozinsky/2017/07/24/how-generation-z-is-shaping-the-change-in-education/#2d4b0c406520

LESSON 83

TEXT US FOR A QUICKER RESPONSE

"We prefer not to email. In fact, when we communicate with other Gen Zers, text is our preferred channel for communication," said Zoe Butchen, a member of the University of Connecticut class of 2022. "From a professional standpoint and with other generations, we know email is the norm, but for us Gen Zers, older generations will get a quicker response if they text us. With Gen Z entering the workforce, there will be a shift from email to text as the primary way to communicate in business."

LESSON 84

IN A TEXT WORLD, A PHONE CALL STANDS OUT

❝Since texting is our norm, receiving a phone call on our birthday or just a spontaneous call from a friend instead of a text or a direct message is unique and appreciated and really stands out in today's social media world," said Zoe Butchen, a member of the University of Connecticut class of 2022. "While Gen Zers use their phone for everything they do, we crave human interaction," said Sophia Kazee, a member of the University of Pittsburgh class of 2021. "I love having a phone call and enjoying a full conversation. Text works for brief and immediate communication, but a phone call allows us to explain things clearly and interact with someone's voice. It is very refreshing in today's Gen Z tech world."

LESSON 85

INSTAGRAM HAS SOME COMPETITION

" Created in 2012, VSCO is a photography app, that is revolutionizing the way Gen Z are taking pictures. The app gives the youth a chance to take professional quality photographs all from their smartphone," reports Immersive Youth Marketing.[76] "VSCO is similar to Instagram and it's starting to gain some real traction with Gen Z," said Zoe Butchen," a member of the University of Connecticut class of 2022. "It is for the artsier photos and has more editing features." Derek Drotman, a member of the Penn State class of 2020 added, "It's more popular and trending among Gen Z girls and is a good app to create an album from a vacation or a special event."

---

76. Brands Doing It Right: Gen Z Loves VSCO Photo Editing App. Retrieved from http://www.immersiveyouthmarketing.com/blog/brands-doing-it-right-gen-z-loves-vsco-photo-editing-app

LESSON 86

TECH DRIVES OUR GEN Z WAY OF SHOPPING

❝ Generation Z grew up during the most accelerated and game-changing periods of technological advancements in human history," writes Ryan Jenkins.[77] With that, it should not be a surprise that the CEO of a mobile marketing provider commented, "They're (Gen Z) increasingly looking for more interactive and personalized ways to shop, with online platforms like search engines, social media and ecommerce marketplaces changing the game for these digitally-savvy consumers and the retail world at-large."[78] Antonia Attardo, a member of the Rutgers University class of 2019, emphasized that, "Technology has completely changed the traditional purchase funnel making it more difficult for marketers to target us. From influencers on YouTube who promote specific clothing or beauty products to Gen Z friends who share brand and retail promotions and special offers, we rely on technology as well as our social media channels and compelling content from brands and other sources to influence our ultimate purchase."

---

77. Jenkins, R. (n.d.). How Generation Z Uses Technology and Social Media. Retrieved from http://blog.ryan-jenkins.com/how-generation-z-uses-technology-and-social-media

78. If You're Looking to Attract Gen Z, Technology Is the Way. (2018, June 18). Retrieved from https://csnews.com/if-youre-looking-attract-gen-z-technology-way

LESSON 87

WE HAVE A TWITCH

M ove over actors, athletes and artists, there is a whole new army of influencers influencing Gen Z thanks to Twitch and the rising popularity of eSports. "Twitch, the online live streaming video platform for video gamers is huge and only getting bigger as eSports evolves and grows," said Thomas Saacks, a member of the class of 2022 at Calvert Hall College High School. "With that, there is a whole new set of influencers, specifically gaming influencers with massive followings such as Tyler "Ninja" Blevins who many of us are following." Jake Panus, a member of the class of 2022 at Fairfield Ludlowe High School added, "Fortnite is very, very popular with me and my friends and equally popular among boys and girls especially now that we can play it on our mobile phones. It is an easy way to connect with your friends while doing something that is fun and challenging at the same time. It is highly addicting and engaging."

LESSON 88

UBER US

"We are the first generation that grew up on shared services like Uber and Lyft. While other generations may waste their time waiting for a taxi, we want things on our time at our location. It's why we even like Uber Eats. With one swipe of the app, we can order food and it gets delivered anywhere and anytime based on what we requested," said Derek Drotman, a member of the Penn State class of 2020. "Services like Uber are our way of life." As companies and brands look to engage Gen Z, they should explore the shared service model that is so appealing to Gen Zers and could potentially satisfy other needs and wants of this generation.

LESSON 89

DELIVER US IMMEDIACY LIKE AMAZON

"Having grown up on Amazon, we place a premium on immediacy. We intentionally don't plan for many things because we know that Amazon or other services can deliver it to us the same day or overnight. We would never consider wasting our time standing on line at the college book store when we can order all our books through Amazon and receive them within 24 hours. Even if we pay a few extra dollars, we place a premium on immediacy and saving time," said Derek Drotman, a member of the Penn State class of 2020. At the workplace or with products and services, Gen Zers prioritize immediacy. If you can deliver what they want faster, they will value and reward you for it.

LESSON 90

MORE OPTIONS ARE BETTER WHEN IT COMES TO TECH

We can never have enough apps or technology. "Endless options for apps and tech allows us to break from conformity and personalize our choices. It allows us to self-identify and in the process, figure out who we are faster," said Christian Glew, a 2018 graduate of the University of Alabama. "I use four different apps just for editing images and that does not include Instagram," commented Sophia Kazee, a member of the University of Pittsburgh class of 2021. "While VSCO is my preferred app for editing photos, I use Lightroom and Darkroom, and Facetune is another popular photo editing app. For Gen Zers, you can never have enough apps and we love options and choices when it comes to customizing our use of technology."

LESSON 91

EDITING IS A PASSION

" While we like immediacy and speed, we invest an extraordinary amount of time editing our content, especially photos, before we post. It's why apps like VSCO are becoming popular," said Derek Drotman, a member of the Penn State class of 2020. "Nothing is unedited in our Gen Z world. We will edit an image of a slice of pizza until we believe it is the greatest photo of a slice of pizza that has ever been taken. It's why 'food porn' is so popular with our generation."

Shelby Fong, a member of the Rutgers University class of 2019, added, "we also are well aware that producing and distributing content that is edited in a quality manner leads to a consistently aesthetic feed which will catch the eye of marketers as we apply for internships or campus ambassador positions." While it is common knowledge that Gen Z takes an endless amount of photo and selfies using their mobile phones, where they are spending quality time is in editing those images before they distribute via their owned media channels and share with their followers. A brand that understands just how important editing is to Gen Z will create a peer-to-peer editing platform or campaign that will truly engage this coveted audience.

LESSON 92

TECHNOLOGY DOES NOT INTIMIDATE US

While previous generations have kicked and screamed when they had to adopt and adapt to new technology or an update on their mobile phone or computer, Gen Z welcomes and embraces the opportunity to meet and learn about new technology, apps and digital tools that will allow their work and social lives to proceed faster and more efficiently. "We are not intimidated at all by technology. We grew up on it and it's just second nature to us," said Austin Sommerer, a 2017 graduate of Penn State University. "There is such a generation gap when it comes to technology. Unlike our parents, Gen Zers seek out new technologies and we quickly want to understand and adopt the latest innovations if we see that they will enhance our way of living, working and socializing."

PART VII

PEEPING THE GEN Z TWEET ON TRENDS & TOPICS

LESSON 93

FAMILY, HOME & CHILDREN CAN WAIT...FOR NOW

Like millennials, it appears Gen Z will not follow the traditional path of older generations of graduating from high school or college, getting a job to pay the bills, getting married, starting a family and buying a home with a white picket fence. A 2018 story captured the trend by writing, "Long ago, marriage was, for the most part, an economic arrangement. This later evolved into a way for people to express their love and commitment to each other. Marriage may be shifting again as Millennials (those born in the 1980's and 1990's) are either not marrying at all or marrying much later. At this point in time, the median age at first marriage is 27 for women and 29 for men. This is up about 7 years since the 1960's and may be slowly climbing."[79] In a story in USA Today, Michael Woods of generational research firm, 747 insights, commented, "Gen Z will likely follow suit with Millennials, who have postponed many of the traditional milestones such as buying a home, getting married, and even having children."[80] Gen Z is prioritizing unique experiences, travel and getting a job not just to pay the bills, but so they can flourish, learn and evolve as unique individuals. "My parents probably think I have a very non-traditional approach to my first decade after college," commented Sabrina Araullo, a 2018 Montclair State University graduate. "Me and my friends have different aspirations

79. Feuerman, M. (2018, April 10). More Millennials Are Choosing to Not Get Married. Retrieved from https://www.verywellmind.com/millennials-and-marriage-the-state-of-their-unions-4136853

80. Generation Z predicts the future: America's kids explain love, marriage and gender roles. (2018, June 19). Retrieved from https://www.wfmynews2.com/article/news/nation-now/generation-z-predicts-the-future-americas-kids-explain-love-marriage-and-gender-roles/465-dc3c1414-d182-4f7e-b860-1e968b4679d2

than starting a family and gaining a mortgage. We will get there, but give us time as we want to explore the world on our time and at our own pace."

LESSON 94

WE PLAN FOR SPONTANEITY

"Other than scheduled activities like work, we are a generation that is seeking spontaneous experiences. I never know where the next text message may take me, so I always have an on-the-go bag in my car. One moment, I could be getting out of work and two hours later I could be 75 miles away at a beach house socializing with friends until I need to get back to work a couple of days later," said Hailey Winnicky, East Stroudsburg University class of 2019. Apps like Find My Friends from Apple have not only empowered Gen Z to "plan" for spontaneous meet-ups but have increased their popularity with this generation. Forbes captured it well when they wrote, "Gen Z is a social generation and social apps are the norms on their smartphones. They want to interact with the people in their social circles, but more importantly, they want to expand those circles with fresh news faces from all around the world."[81]

81. Noel, M. (2018, May 18). Hey Facebook, Gen Z Is Finding New Ways To Connect Socially. Retrieved from https://www.forbes.com/sites/marcusnoel/2018/05/18/hey-facebook-gen-z-is-finding-new-ways-to-connect-socially/#7c0f7e5d1468

LESSON 95

WE LOVE CUSTOMIZED CLASSES

Whether you call it personalization or customization, Gen Zers love it at work, play and even at the gym. "It's more of an enjoyable experience to go to Soul Cycle, Peleton, Pure Barre and workout with a group of like-minded individuals for 45-60 minutes than going to a massive gym," said Brooke Stern, a member of the Cornell University class of 2019. "It provides a personalization to my exercise routine and it allows me to pursue my fitness passions."

LESSON 96

EVEN WHEN WE ARE
RELAXING WE ARE ENGAGED

"Unlike previous generations, we never relax. Even when we are sitting down watching a movie or video on our laptop, we are multi-screening and multi-tasking. I can't remember a time when I was just sitting idle. Gen Z is engaged 24/7 and we always need to be productive," said Derek Drotman, a member of the Penn State class of 2020.

LESSON 97

NOT ALL GEN ZERS ARE THE SAME

Born in the age of technology, there are distinct differences between the older and younger members of Generation Z when you consider the oldest are already 23 and have started working full-time and the youngest are only going into first grade. "Gen Zers my age, have only known smartphones. As technology changes exponentially, so will the change in Gen Zers depending on when they were born," said Thomas Saacks, a member of the class of 2022 at Calvert Hall College High School. "Technology continues to be introduced to Gen Zers at a younger and younger age so younger Gen Zers will adopt and adapt much more quickly to new apps and tech and will crave innovation that transforms their lives even when they are still only in middle school and high school."

LESSON 98

RETRO IS RELEVANT

Vinyl records, thrift shops, hand written notes, real cameras (not smartphones), a phone call on your birthday – these are all things Gen Z considers "retro" which they take notice of in their hi-tech way of living. "Living in a 24/7 tech and social media world, what is most disruptive is what we would consider retro products or retro forms of communication," said Summer Beal, a 2018 graduate of East Stroudsburg University. "A phone call or a hand-written note will stop us in our tracks, take notice and even share with our followers on social media." Keep that in mind brand marketers – as you develop tech-forward marketing campaigns, a little bit of "retro" may disrupt the marketplace and set you apart from your competitors.

LESSON 99

WE CAN BE MOODY

" Gen Zers have developed completely new dialects and methods of indicating mood though text that has never been seen before," said Christian Glew, a 2018 graduate of the University of Alabama. "We can be sarcastic or mocking depending on how we text using a combination of capital letters, ellipses and a series of periods." Christina Hamdan, a member of the University of Delaware class of 2019, added, "Generation Z prioritizes the use of punctuation marks, upper and lower-case letters and other symbols to express our mood more than any previous generation. We grew up texting and the way we text is another nuance to our unique language and our way with words, symbols, numbers and more."

LESSON 100

DISCONNECTING IS IMPORTANT TO US

"We find ourselves so connected to technology that we seek out places and times when we can completely disconnect from social media, our phones and all of our apps," said Austin Sommerer, a 2017 graduate of Penn State University. "When my friends and I socialize and get together for dinner, we have started stacking our phones in the middle of the table to force ourselves to socialize face-to-face in conversation. The person who checks their phone first pays the tab." Mike Morra, a 2017 graduate of Manhattan College added, "I have a fascination with this movement away from social media and technology. There is this moving desire for more immersive experiences." Marketers should look at Gen Zers disconnecting from their phones as a potential opportunity to connect with them by facilitating opportunities to disconnect and connect with others via H.I. – Human Interaction. A digital detox or a social media siesta is not just a phenomenon with Gen Zers in the United States. According to a survey of more than 1,000 students across the United Kingdom by student marketing agency Seed, 77% said they would definitely take a digital detox or consider doing a no-social-media-month.[82] Marketers and brands must take notice of Gen Zers disconnecting from social media and technology and offer relevant and meaningful alternative programming.

---

82. Cescau, K. (2018, July 6). From digital detox dreamers to exploring unfiltered worlds, what marketers need to know about Gen Z. Retrieved from https://www.campaignlive.com/article/digital-detox-dreamers-exploring-unfiltered-worlds-marketers-need-know-gen-z/1486874

LESSON 101

WE WILL CHANGE THE WORLD

From climate control to gun laws, Gen Z is not afraid to take a stand when it comes to political or societal issues. "With school shootings happening too regularly, we are openly discussing a variety of issues and creating a Gen Z movement. I participated in my first march this year and it was loud, empowering and full of energy and I can't wait to do it again with other students from my generation," said Jake Panus, a member of the 2022 class at Fairfield Ludlowe High School. Christina Hamdan, a member of the University of Delaware class of 2019, added, "Our generation takes the initiative to get involved with issues whether nationally or locally. At my university, we just developed a club to shed light on issues such as mental health. By being proactive participants, we are making an impact at the local level and it's a cause I feel passionate about that I want to lend my voice to. Our generation is being heard for sure. Gen Z will change the world."

FINAL THOUGHTS

As Christina Hamdan stated in the final lesson in this book, "Gen Z will change the world." Generation Z is already transforming the world it at a faster rate than anyone could have predicted.

Time featured five Gen Zers on their cover in March 2018 with the headline, "ENOUGH." following the shooting at Stoneman Douglas High School, in Parkland, Florida. Several year's earlier Canada's national magazine, *Maclean's*, introduced that country to these transformers with the cover headline, "Are You Ready For Generation Z: They're smarter than boomers and way more ambitious than millennials. Brace yourself for the ultimate generation war." As this book is being published, the Gen Z movement is in the process of motivating elected officials to lower the voting age to 16 in local and federal elections including for president. Can you imagine the influence they will have on the 2020 presidential election?

As I referenced earlier in this book, I "listened" to more than 50 Gen Zers ranging in ages from 13 to 23 from Maryland to Mississippi and Connecticut to California. On the young side, these Gen Zers were preparing to start high school while the older Gen Zers were starting their first full-time job after graduating college. I "listened" to Gen Zers and that would be the one final lesson that I would share with corporate America, brand marketers and media – "Listen To Gen Z!"

If you really listen to Gen Z today, tomorrow, next year and 10 years from now, you will learn how to be more efficient, effective and engaging in whatever it is that you do. I predict that Gen Z will not only change the world, but they will transform technology, communications, media, social media, digital media, content, the workplace, corporations, society, norms, culture, mindsets and

FINAL THOUGHTS • 127

you – but only if you take the time to listen to all that Generation Z has to offer the world.

ABOUT THE AUTHOR

Since 2013, Mark Beal has served as an adjunct professor in the School of Communication at Rutgers University in New Brunswick, New Jersey. He also teaches and collaborates with students at Montclair State University. He has designed and taught 300 and 400 level courses including Media, Marketing and Communication; Leadership in Groups & Organizations; Principles of Public Relations; and Message Design for Public Relations. During that time, he has taught more than 1,000 students and mentored many more across the nation. It was these students who inspired Mark to write his first book, *101 Lessons They Never Taught You In College*, which was published in 2017 and is available for purchase on Amazon. The book serves as a guide for students as they navigate the transition from college to a career. In 2018, he collaborated with many of his students to author *101 Lessons They Never Taught You In High School About Going To College*.

Mark brings his 101 lessons to life via his podcast series, 101 Lessons in Leadership. In each podcast episode, Mark interviews a leader and delves into the mentors who inspired them as well as the lessons in leadership and life that they share with their current followers. The podcast episodes can be listened to for free by simply going to www.101lessonspodcast.com.

Aside from teaching, Mark has developed and executed award-winning public relations and marketing campaigns for some of the most recognizable brands for the past 25 years. His marketing work has taken him to the Olympic Games, Super Bowl, World Series, US Open and "on tour" with The Rolling Stones.

Mark received his BA in journalism from Rutgers University and his MA in communications from Kent State University. He lives in Toms River, NJ with his wife, Michele, where they enjoy boating, paddle boarding, cycling, running, swimming, tennis and golf. They have three children, Drew, Meghan, Summer, a daughter-in-law, Huda, and two grandchildren, Luke and Marc.

Twitter: @markbealpr
Email: markbeal@markbealmedia.com
Phone: +1.848.992.0391

62948392R00084

Made in the USA
Middletown, DE
26 August 2019